Deliver Us II:

Discovering Your Idols on the Path to the Promised Land

Deliver Us II:

Discovering Your Idols on the Path to the Promised Land

by Don Umphrey

CASA

CHRISTIANS AGAINST SUBSTANCE ABUSE
CHRISTIANS AGAINST SEXUAL ADDICTION

CASA is an international program focusing on Christian perspectives on addiction recovery. CASA provides support and literature to groups that meet in churches and penal institutions. Visit www.AskCASA.com for more information.

Quarry Press • PO Box 181736 • Dallas, Texas 75218
quarrypress@msn.com • www.quarrypressbooks.com

Printed in the United States of America.

Editor, Timothy S. Miller
Biblical Editor, Wayne Williams
Copy Editor, Susie Meyer
Book and cover design and layout, Angie Maddox

ISBN: 978-1-937766-06-1

Library of Congress Control Number: 2012906411

Dedicated

to the

Glory of God

Table of Contents

For I do not want you to be ignorant of the fact, brothers, that our forefathers were all under the cloud and that they all passed through the sea. They were all baptized into Moses in the cloud and in the sea. They all ate the same spiritual food and drank the same spiritual drink; for they drank from the spiritual rock that accompanied them, and that rock was Christ. Nevertheless, God was not pleased with most of them; their bodies were scattered over the desert.

Now these things occurred as examples to keep us from setting our hearts on evil things as they did. Do not be idolaters, as some of them were; as it is written: "The people sat down to eat and drink and got up to indulge in pagan revelry." We should not commit sexual immorality, as some of them did—and in one day twenty-three thousand of them died. We should not test the Lord, as some of them did—and were killed by snakes. And do not grumble, as some of them did—and were killed by the destroying angel.

These things happened to them as examples and were written down as warnings for us, on whom the fulfillment of the ages has come.

I Corinthians 10:1-11

Introduction

Living in a Texas prison is what Randall Lee Church knew best. He was incarcerated for 27½ years after killing a man during a drunken dispute over $97. He was 18 when that happened.

With his release date approaching in 2011, Randall didn't believe fellow inmates who warned he would be in for a shock after leaving prison to enter "the free world."

He now understands the validity of those cautions.

Here's what he said about his 99 days of freedom: "Everything had gone fast-forward without me. I didn't know how to use computers or cell phones or the internet. It was so overwhelming. I was constantly embarrassed by simple things I just didn't know."[1]

"The weirdest thing was walking into a store, like Walmart, and have parents hide their children from me, like I was supposed to jump at them."[2] I wrote a letter to Randall to ask why he had that impression. He wrote back that it was because of the tattoos on his arms and neck.

That may be true. There are, however, many heavily tattooed people in our society, including any number of professional athletes who regularly appear on our television screens. It is possible that what Randall saw in the eyes of others was a reflection of his own insecurities from trying to get along in an alien world that had moved forward without him.

Out of frustration within a few months of his release, Randall poured gasoline through the window of an empty house, according to a newspaper report.[3] He then tossed in some burning rags and paper towels before leaving. "It was my ticket to go back (to prison) if I wanted," he told a newspaper reporter.[4]

Three days later, he redeemed that ticket by visiting a restaurant and eating what he knew would be his "last supper" before returning to a life behind bars. It included a hamburger, French fries, and two chocolate shakes.

When it came time to pay, Randall confessed to the waitress that he lacked sufficient funds. He was carrying only 31 cents. He asked her to call the police. The restaurant manager came to his table and told Randall he was free to leave if he promised to never come back. He then confessed that he'd committed a crime.

He later told police about the arson. Randall also told officers he wanted to return to his work as a janitor inside the McConnell Prison Unit in Beeville, Texas, a position that had allowed him to have all of the ice and soda pop he wanted during the summers.

He was sent to a different prison unit with the possibility of a second parole at some point in the future. According to the newspaper, it was not clear if his new prison job would include ice and soft drinks.[5]

Do you identify with Randall?

I certainly do. In fact, I used his story here because it is a nutshell version of a plight common to humanity, Christians in particular.

Why do I single out fellow believers? We understand that we reside in a fallen world and live with the promise of an eternal future much better than our present lives.

In the meantime, though, we grow accustomed to living with the chains that bind, the product of our culture and our own choices in life. Though God's Word warns us about them or others may try to caution, our shackles remain invisible to us.

We strive toward the true freedom offered by Jesus Christ, but it is difficult—daunting, even—to make the changes that will enable us to do this. Like Adam and Eve suddenly realizing they were naked (see Genesis 3:1-13) or Randall in Walmart, we feel a need to hide or retreat to the familiar.

Inside, there's also a constant gnawing telling us that we could do better if we only tried harder, but we're never successful in getting it all together.

If you limp along long enough with a large pebble in your shoe, you'll get used to it.

Spiritually speaking, what is causing you to limp along life's journey?

You may venture out toward the promise of that ultimate freedom. When you do, though, your own versions of Randall's ice and soft drinks will beckon you back.

AN OLD PROBLEM

In some ways, our situation is parallel to that of God's people, the Hebrews (also called the Israelites and children of Israel), who served as slaves in Egypt more than 3,000 years ago. Here's what

God said about their circumstances: "I've taken a good, long look at the affliction of my people in Egypt. I've heard their cries for deliverance from their slave masters; I know all about their pain" (Exodus 3:7, *The Message*).

Moses was chosen by God to act as His spokesman with the Hebrews and lead them out of Egypt. "They marched out boldly in full view of all the Egyptians" (Numbers 33:3). Two and a half months after their departure, however, these liberated slaves started talking about the "good ol' days" back in Egypt. Several weeks later, they were worshipping an Egyptian idol.

Though the idols have changed since the time of Moses, idolatry hasn't. Our culture is rife with opportunities to bow down to any number of idols. We try to hide behind them to cover up our nakedness.

My turning to alcohol to do for me what I seemingly could not do for myself made it abundantly clear that I worshipped an idol that could be found in brown, green, and clear bottles.

Do you recognize any idols in your own life?

It is so easy to fall short of the biblical admonition, "Throw off everything that hinders and the sin that so easily entangles, and let us run with perseverance the race marked out for us" (Hebrews 12:1).

That race is our life's journey, which is equivalent to the Israelites crossing the desert. Their destination was the Promised Land, and our Promised Land is heaven. In this volume, we will look at parallels between our trip and theirs.

Part One of this book examines the land of slavery. The idols of ancient Egypt are not so different from those found in our own culture. We may not even be aware that parts of our identities are based on the idols we carry with us. We also have a way of getting bogged down by idols we've acquired in vain attempts to fill the emptiness inside where God belongs. Part One will help to identify your idols.

Part Two is the journey away from the land of slavery toward our Promised Land while we are attempting to be solely dependent on our Lord God to provide for us and lead the way. We will make several stops along the path followed by the Israelites to gain spiritual insights. We also will discover that we continue to carry idols that we didn't recognize earlier.

As you continue reading, you'll find plenty of biblical examples and quotations, the insights of other authors, and illustrations from my slavery to alcoholism.

Part I: The Land of Slavery

The Egyptians came to dread the Israelites

and worked them ruthlessly.

They made their lives bitter with hard labor

in brick and mortar and with

all kinds of work in the fields; in all their hard

labor the Egyptians used them ruthlessly.

Exodus 1:12-14

CHAPTER ONE

A Decision

Pulling the door shut behind me on a cold night in January, I entered The Golden Rooster, a bar located in Farmington, Michigan, the suburb northwest of Detroit where I grew up. It was dimly lit and filled with smoke. Carly Simon's "You're So Vain" blared from the jukebox to join simultaneous loud conversations and occasional outbursts of laughter.

I made my way between tables of fellow customers mostly in their twenties. The bartender nodded as I approached.

"Diet Pepsi."

He cocked his head slightly and looked at me with skepticism. "Diet Pepsi?"

I nodded.

"With nothing in it?"

"Right."

"You don't want a beer or something?"

"I don't drink."

His expression darkened. "I don't trust people who don't drink. What's wrong with you?"

I shrugged.

Doing nothing to mask his mocking expression, he served up my diet soda. Then I headed toward the table where my best friend, Rich, and others were talking and drinking from pitchers of beer.

My lone sibling is my sister, Jan, but if I could have picked someone to be my brother, it would have been Rich. We'd been buddies since we first met at Farmington Junior High. Throughout adolescence, we'd played football, hunted, fished, and chased girls together. We knew each other's secrets.

The first time I got drunk, it was with Rich during my junior year of high school. A guy in my chemistry class with a fake ID bought us a pint each of whiskey and vodka. We drank this stuff one winter night while sitting in my dad's car parked in front of Rich's house.

We staggered into his house and got in trouble because his mom was still awake. It could have been much worse except that his dad was a sound sleeper. After I got home with a terrible hangover the next morning, my parents found out about our venture into under-age drinking.

Rich and I had learned our lesson. It was nearly a year before we got drunk again, and from then on, we took more precautions about being caught.

Sitting together in the bar that night, we were both 27. Gambling on horses and games of pinochle, barhopping, and heavy drinking (until recently for me) were a part of our routine. Of course, the pursuit of women continued, some of whom were topless dancers.

I consumed several soft drinks that night, and Rich drank about as many beers as he would normally.

A few hours later, Rich had his arm around me, and his leg was draped over mine beneath the table. Our faces were about six inches apart as he explained something that at the moment was a matter of great importance to him. Without having imbibed in some "social lubricant" myself, Rich's reasoning didn't make a lot of sense to me.

I surmised that we'd enjoyed many such conversations in the past. Now, though, I came to a painful realization: There was a disconnect between us resulting from my not drinking.

Would I do something to patch up this uncomfortable situation? A double Scotch on the rocks? A few beers?

DELUSIONS PRESIDE

A little over two months earlier, the phobias and anxieties that had plagued me for several years finally had taken over. One morning while vainly attempting to focus on my work as a newspaper editor, I felt panicky and ran into the men's room. Staring into the mirror, it seemed as if I could see within the confines of my skull. Where my brain was supposed to be located, I saw a mass of spoiled scrambled eggs. My legs trembled, and I grabbed the sink to keep from falling to the floor.

It sounds like a bad trip on LSD, but it wasn't. In fact, I never used that drug. My illegal drug consumption had been confined to smoking marijuana about a half dozen times and swallowing some "uppers" and "downers" a few times in college. "Old dependable" for me was the drug that could be purchased legally just about anywhere: alcohol.

To ward off the insanity after trembling in front of the mirror, I ran back to my desk and took out one of the beers I'd hidden in a drawer. I hurried back to the restroom, held it to my lips with shaking hands, and guzzled it down.

During the next few days, I had more panic attacks followed immediately by doses of whiskey. Even though I had reached that point of desperation, it was still not clear to me that my fears of impending doom were compounding while alcohol was having diminishing effects in its ability to calm me down.

It got to the point where suicide seemed like the only way out. That's not the bitter ending I wanted, but I didn't know where else to turn.

Finally, after getting little sleep on the nights of November 4 and 5, I got out of bed early on the morning of November 6 in the midst of the mother of all anxiety attacks. I started chugging beers. Still frantic, I turned to straight Scotch. Still no help.

Barely resisting the thought of instantaneous self-destruction, I called the woman I'd been dating and spilled out my dilemma. She left work, picked me up, and we drove to a mental hospital that had been recommended.

Note that I did not seek a treatment center for alcoholics. Based on what I'd learned from visiting a psychologist and reading psychology books, I had long assumed I was mentally ill. A solution to my problems always eluded me, though it seemed to be just around the corner via more sessions with the psychologist or between the pages of the latest self-help book.

As the fog started to clear after a few days in the hospital, I became acquainted with some of my fellow patients. One of them was "Ron," a man with a great sense of humor about 15 years my senior who worked as a trash collector. We became friends and compared notes on why we'd each landed there.

Ron was going into delirium tremens when taken to the hospital. He said that upon his discharge, he planned to attend a program that helped alcoholics. He wondered if my problems might stem from alcohol and whether I might benefit from such a program.

We had many conversations about these possibilities. Before I left the hospital after two weeks, Ron and I made a pact that we would each try to not drink anything containing alcohol and that we would attend recovery meetings utilizing the 12 steps.

How ironic that alcohol turned out to be the problem. During my senior year of high school, I started viewing it as *the* solution. A few beers before a party or dance transformed me from shy and stand-offish to the party animal I wanted to be. Alcohol seemed to be my key to popularity. I went away to college thinking it could solve any problem I might encounter. I still clung to this notion a decade later as I chugged straight Scotch in the parking lot of the mental hospital just before admitting myself.

By the time I sat down with Rich at the bar that night, I had attended several recovery meetings. Still not connecting my huge alcohol intake with my deteriorating mental state, I was not sure I really belonged. The people at those meetings said they wanted to stop drinking. In and of itself, that was not my goal. I wanted to stop feeling miserable and being a slave to anxieties and phobias. I did take hope, however, in hearing their testimonies.

As the evening wore on at the bar, I was stone-cold sober and feeling pretty empty. It was obvious that I had to take action. One possibility was to order a drink. The other was to remember my pledge to Ron about not drinking. I chose the latter when I left Rich and the others in The Golden Rooster and went home long before last call.

I made the right choice that night. There have been occasions, however, when I decided to do the wrong thing, despite possible negative consequences.

Have you ever made a conscious decision to do the wrong thing? If yes, what was it? If no, are you sure?

Earlier, I mentioned that Rich and I knew each other's secrets, but this was not completely true. He didn't know about the anxieties, phobias, and fears of impending doom with which I'd been living. I was afraid that such disclosures would make me seem like less of a man. But after I had been sober for a few months, I told Rich what had been going on inside of me. He was pretty shocked but came to understand. Rich and I are still friends today.

I continued going to the recovery meetings, though not completely sure that such a program was a fit for me. Reading through the literature of that group, though, I ran across a first-person story that told about a man who experienced the same effects from drinking that I did. He, too, had been paralyzed by fears of impending doom. With ongoing sobriety, however, he reached a point where those mental problems no longer controlled his life.

Tears came to my eyes as I read his story. Finally, I identified and was able to name my idol, the source of my problems. From then on, I had no questions as to whether I belonged in the recovery group. Like the man in the story, my fears gradually faded away, providing me with a new life beyond my greatest expectations.

As of this writing, the last time I bowed down to the idol of alcohol was in the parking lot of the mental hospital on November 6, 1973. These years of sobriety as a new creation in Jesus Christ are all through His grace. However, my personal battles continue as I discover old idols I've been carrying with me all along while also encountering possible new ones.

What personal battles are you fighting?

Are they the result of idolatry?

CHAPTER TWO

Straddling the Fence

Will you worship God or god? This contrast is spelled out in the First Commandment which starts out, "I am the Lord your God" (Exodus 20:2).

God is "Our Father" (Matthew 6:9). We are made in His image (Genesis 1:26-27). He loves us, knows the best for us, and will guide us. To be true to our innermost selves, we will seek God and follow the admonition of Moses, "Hear, O Israel: The Lord our God, the Lord is one. Love the Lord your God with all your heart and with all your soul and with all your strength" (Deuteronomy 6:4-5), known to Jewish worshipers as the Shema.[1]

The First Commandment concludes, "You shall have no other gods before me" (Exodus 20:3).

These lower-case-g gods are the same as idols, and they include anyone or anything that will lead us in a direction away from our Father. There are many gods, but only one God. This is why the Shema begins with "Hear, O Israel: The Lord our God, the Lord is one" (Deuteronomy 6:4).

There were many gods in ancient Egypt. The conflict that unfolded between Moses and Pharaoh, the king of Egypt, demonstrates the stark contrast in life's direction that naturally follows from choosing either God or gods/idols.

In those moments of shock and awe as Moses beheld the sight of the burning bush, the Lord revealed the plan of deliverance for His children in Egypt and the role Moses would play in their liberation.

> *I have come down to rescue them from the hand of the Egyptians and to bring them up out of that land into a good and spacious land, a land flowing with milk and honey... And now the cry of the Israelites has reached me, and I have seen the way the Egyptians are oppressing them. So now, go. I am sending you to Pharaoh to bring my people the Israelites out of Egypt (Exodus 3:8-10).*

Having been a prince there, Moses was very familiar not only with the political and religious climate of Egypt but also with the nature of his fellow Israelites. Undoubtedly, he recognized the enormity of the task God had set before him. Perhaps this is why Moses initially balked when receiving his marching orders.

Moses also knew that Egyptian rulers could be heartless. If it had been up to the Pharaoh ruling Egypt at the time of his birth 80 years earlier, Moses would have drowned in the Nile River, been devoured by a crocodile, or both. By order of that tyrant, such was the fate of Hebrew sons being born at that time.

Instead, Moses was spared when his mother placed him in a

basket among the reeds along the shore of the Nile River. It was spotted by a daughter of Pharaoh who'd gone to bathe. Sending a slave girl to retrieve the basket, the princess felt compassion for the crying infant she recognized as a Hebrew.

Watching from a distance, Moses's sister approached. "Shall I go and get one of the Hebrew women to nurse the baby for you?" (Exodus 2:7) The princess agreed and, in fact, paid Moses's birth mother to nurture the baby. Later, Moses was adopted into the royal household as the son of the princess. This allowed him to spend the first 40 years of his life as a part of Egyptian royalty.

Despite this elevated lifestyle, Moses was sensitive to the plight of his own people. This became apparent when he killed an Egyptian who was mistreating a Hebrew slave. Hiding the body, Moses thought no one else knew about this act but soon found that word had spread. To escape execution at the order of Pharaoh, Moses made a hasty exit from Egypt. He spent the next 40 years as a shepherd in Midian.

It was then that the Lord spoke to him from the burning bush.

Voicing his reluctance to the Lord to undertake the task set out before him, Moses observed that he was not an eloquent speaker. The Lord then said that Moses's brother, Aaron, could serve as a spokesman for them.

In the four decades since Moses had left Egypt, a different Pharaoh had ascended to the throne. Appearing before this Pharaoh for the first time, the brothers stated, "This is what the Lord, the God of Israel, says: 'Let my people go, so that they may hold a festival to me in the desert'" (Exodus 5:1).

Pharaoh answered, "Who is the Lord, that I should obey him

and let Israel go? I do not know the Lord and I will not let Israel go" (Exodus 5:2).

Of course, Pharaoh did not know the Lord God because he thought he himself was God. He was one in a long line of Pharaohs who believed he had the dual responsibilities of serving simultaneously as both God and king.

MYTHOLOGY IN ACTION

Here is the Egyptian myth that accounted for why Pharaoh thought he was God: [2]

Much earlier, the ruler god, Osiris, was happily married to his sister, Isis. Their jealous brother, known as either Set or Seth, killed Osiris and scattered pieces of his body throughout Egypt. Isis and others searched the entirety of the country and discovered all the body parts but one. Isis then reassembled the pieces of the corpse, and this was said to have accounted for Osiris becoming Egypt's first mummy.

This wasn't enough for Isis as she then took action to become a mommy.

That one missing piece of Osiris was a part that would enable him to become a daddy, but it was nowhere to be found. This is because Set had tossed it into the Nile River, where it was devoured by a fish.

Undaunted, Isis fashioned a new member and attached it to the corpse of Osiris before breathing life into him. The two of them went on to discover that the replacement part was quite functional, and she became pregnant, giving birth to the god, Horus.

Osiris then passed into the afterlife, where he reigned as the god of the dead. As such, he was depicted in Egyptian art as a mummified king with either black or green skin. "Every aspect of burial and mummification came to be linked to the mythology of Osiris," according to Egyptologist Geraldine Pinch.[3]

Horus, the offspring of Osiris and Isis, was the god of sky and war. He usually was depicted as a man with the head of a falcon.

Each successive Pharaoh, including the one standing before Moses and Aaron, was thought to be the personification of Horus while living[4] and Osiris after he died.[5]

With the worship of some 80 gods, the ancient Egyptians "were just about the most polytheistic people known from the ancient world," according to author John J. Davis.[6] The gods and goddesses of Egypt were associated with aspects of nature and various animals that were held as sacred, including the cow, dog, cat, vulture, falcon, hippo, crocodile, some species of fish, and smaller creatures such as the frog and the scarab beetle.[7]

Writing about the roots of the ancient Egyptian religion, author Bruce Feiler observed, "They worshiped the sun, because it's powerful. They worshiped the water, because it gave them irrigation. They worshiped the crocodile, because it was strong. They looked at nature and took their religious views from it."[8]

Why is it important for us to know about these lower-case-*g* gods? The children of Israel had been influenced greatly by the Egyptian culture in which they'd been enslaved for four centuries. Not only were they slaves in the physical sense, but they also were spiritual slaves because of their idolatry with the gods of Egypt. (See Joshua 24:14, Jeremiah 2:5-8, and Ezekiel 20:7.)

Despite this idolatry, there is plenty of biblical evidence that the Hebrews maintained their belief in God whom their forefathers, the Patriarchs, had served. For example, the slaves had cried out to God for help (Exodus 2:23), and Moses had been told by God to identify Him to the children of Israel as "The Lord, the God of your fathers—the God of Abraham, the God of Isaac and the God of Jacob" (Exodus 3:15). (For additional examples, see the endnote[9].) By believing in the God of their forefathers while also practicing Egyptian idolatry, the children of Israel had their feet planted firmly in opposing theological camps. To one degree or another, the same is true for professing Christians today as we are influenced by the culture in which we reside.

Is it possible you are serving both God and gods? Give examples.

THE SPIRITUAL ELEMENT

People at the recovery group told me, "Your sobriety is contingent on your spiritual condition." In short, God both was and is the solution.

I had conflicting thoughts about God and religion. In my immediate past, I thought of Christians as nerds, weaklings, and wimps.

Having professed to be an atheist at the age of 25, I still had grave doubts as to God's existence. Furthermore, if God did exist, why would He care if I stayed sober, particularly after the way I'd behaved during the previous years?

On the other hand, I felt a measure of comfort after hearing that the recovery group was spiritual. A belief in God reminded me of happier times from my childhood and adolescence when I attended church and Sunday school.

I started seeking God in prayer but really wasn't sure if my words were going anywhere beyond the walls and ceiling of my small apartment.

That changed one day, though.

Based on my new spiritual quest, I thought about returning to church. A few blocks from my apartment was a small congregation of the religious group in which I'd grown up. I went there for three consecutive Sundays, but no one talked to me, even though I tried to initiate conversation.

Did God want me to attend a church where pre-membership shunning was practiced? I didn't think so. In prayer, I asked God to direct me to a church where He wanted me to attend, even if it wasn't the religious group in which I'd grown up.

A few days later, my mother called to tell me I'd received an invitation to attend a reunion of people who'd attended Christian-oriented Lipscomb University in Nashville, Tennessee. I had graduated from Lipscomb after being kicked out of Eastern Michigan University by earning a .7 grade point average during a semester of daily drunkenness.

The reunion was to be hosted by a church about 10 miles south of my apartment. I went and really enjoyed it, although none of my former classmates were present.

As I was leaving, I ran into Maurice and Marie Hall, the minister at that church and his wife. After introductions, they asked where I went to church. "Nowhere," I replied. Then I told them that I was an alcoholic and had been in a mental hospital a few months earlier.

Apparently sensing my unease, they replied, "We could use someone like you around here," and encouraged me to visit. I started attending there immediately. I can report now that my meeting with them has impacted the rest of my life, not only spiritually but geographically and professionally.

Having said that, my thoughts and actions after returning to church indicated that like the children of Israel, I was straddling a fence between the prospects of spiritual freedom and my land-of-slavery life.

Recall that I had long thought that only nerds were religious.

On Sunday mornings, I would put on a coat and tie for church but hoped that no one in my apartment complex would see me getting in my car to go there.

In the same vein, the minister took me to a restaurant for lunch one day. Before we started to eat, he reached across the table to take my hands so that we could pray together. As we bowed our heads, I was embarrassed beyond belief. My only prayer was that no one else in the restaurant would see us.

From time to time, I still would visit a strip bar and order soft drinks, sometimes with a friend from the recovery group.

On one occasion, I went by myself for lunch at a nudie bar. To understand what happened next, you need to know that I was 27 and broad-shouldered, stood six feet, two inches, and weighed about 225 pounds. To top this off, I was wearing a Detroit Lions jacket.

One of the strippers asked if I played for the Lions. Of course, I answered, "Yes." This made me the center of attention of several of the young women who were employed at that establishment.

They asked my name, and I answered Paul Naumoff. He was a linebacker on the team.

Next, one of them asked my uniform number. I couldn't remember Naumoff's number, so I told her, "I'll give you a hint. It is in the 50s," because I knew linebackers usually wore a number in that range. As it turned out, he wore number 50.

I can't recall whether I signed any autographs.

If that is not a good enough illustration of how the gods of my past still controlled my mindset during the early days of my sobriety, let me add this postscript: I later bragged about the above incident to the minister and his wife.

As I subsequently have found in my Christian walk, having one foot planted in church and the other in a slave-world culture is not confined to manifesting itself through visits to strip bars. I'm still guilty today, though it shows itself in different ways.

What about you?

Do you truly have both feet planted firmly in Christianity?

CHAPTER THREE

The Heart of the Matter

Though the word "heart" may be found more than 900 times in the Bible, only rarely does it refer to the organ that pumps blood through our bodies. In its figurative usage, the heart is "the seat of affections," "the seat of intellect," or "the innermost being."[1]

Jesus made reference to one's heart when defining the greatest commandment, "Love the Lord your God with all your heart and with all your soul and with all your mind" (Matthew 22:37).

The alternative is to have a deceived heart, which the prophet Isaiah associated with idolatry (Isaiah 44:20, *New American Standard*). I can say for certain that during those years of near daily drunkenness, my heart was deceived, and the deception grew deeper and darker with the passage of time.

In the parable of the sower, Jesus linked a deceived heart to the ultimate source of evil. "The devil comes and takes away the word from their hearts, so that they may not believe and be saved" (Luke 8:12). Satan also is described as the one "who deceives the whole world" (Revelation 12:9, *New American Standard*). His influence may be found behind every lower-case-*g* god/idol.

Since we know that Moses was acting on behalf of God and wanted to liberate the Israelites, we may conclude that Pharaoh was a pawn of Satan in attempting to keep the Hebrews as his slaves.

Pharaoh's culture told him he was God, and with the power that went with that position, there were plenty of seeming up sides for him. His refusal to give up these delusions created mounting problems in his life, as it will in the life of anyone who follows the same path.

When any person claims to be God—in words or deeds, he/she is following Satan.

"You will be like God, knowing good and evil" (Genesis 3:5) was Satan's temptation to Eve in the Garden of Eden. This temptation reflects Satan's attempt to replace God. (See Isaiah 14:12-14 and Revelation 12:3-4, 9. For an in-depth explanation of the way Satan works in the lives of people and what it takes to leave that self-destructive lifestyle for a God-centered life, see *Deliver Us I*.)

With this piece of the puzzle in place, we can see that the Moses-Pharaoh conflict is the same one that you and I face daily. Will we heed the voice of our Creator or the God-pretender, Satan?

It is important for each of us to make up our mind one way or the other. A person can't straddle the fence continually as I did in the early months of my sobriety or as did the children of Israel during their captivity in Egypt. As Jesus said, "No one can serve two masters. Either he will hate the one and love the other, or he will be devoted to the one and despise the other" (Matthew 6:24).

Who wants to be the ventriloquist with you sitting in his lap as the dummy?

Who would want anyone, including the children of Israel, to languish in slavery?

Who would want me to return to the slavery of alcoholism and destroy myself with booze?

The answer to all these questions is Satan. Not only does he want to deceive our hearts, but he'll break them in the process.

In what ways have you been deceived?

What did it take to recognize this deception?

Is it possible that you are still in the midst of self-deception and don't recognize it?

If yes, what gives you that impression?

CHAPTER FOUR

Uncovering Idols

The ancient Egyptians deified crocodiles, which seems mighty strange today. There was a time in my life, however, when I worshipped a stingray. More specifically, it was a Corvette Sting Ray, the model produced from 1963 to 1967.

Growing up in and around Detroit, Michigan, then considered "the automobile capital of the world," Corvettes were the most coveted set of wheels for everyone I knew. This car was sleek, fast, and prestigious. It spoke tons about the ultra-coolness of its driver—at least in my opinion.

The author's classic 1963 Corvette Sting Ray coupe. Note the split rear window, a major distinction between this Sting Ray and later models. Below, the author at age 23 prepares to install a front license plate on this new (to him) car shortly after purchasing it. Check out those white pants.

My earliest memory of being close-up with this sports car was when I visited the home of Carol, my fourth-grade girlfriend for about a week and a half. Sitting in her parents' driveway were a Cadillac and her dad's blue Corvette that had extra lights added to the front and back.

Magazines depicting cars of the future were visible throughout their house. I knew that her father worked for General Motors, but it was decades later when I learned that he had been the chief designer of the first Corvette that came out in 1953, just a few years prior to my visit.

My next brush with a Corvette owner was about three years later. Dewey, the assistant janitor at our junior high, appeared to be the ultimate playboy driving his red Corvette convertible on Grand River Avenue in downtown Farmington.

Going into my senior year of college, I regularly drove a red 1963 Corvette coupe belonging to my friend, Roy. That year's Sting Ray is noteworthy as being the only model with a split rear window. Today, it is highly esteemed by collectors.

I still had the itch to buy my very own Corvette. With college graduation approaching, Roy and I shopped around, and the prospect of being a Corvette owner myself started seeming economically feasible.

We found one like Roy's except that it was green. It looked great for a six-year-old car! The cost was $2,000, a lot of money at that time for a full-time student/part-time lifeguard, but a credit union let me buy it with no money down, and my parents agreed to pay the first three monthly payments of $68.

Driving it away as my very own, I could hardly contain myself. The first chance I got, I took it up through the gears. Wow, what power!

Later that day, though, I felt a hollowness deep inside of me. It formed into a lump that made my throat hurt. I wanted to cry but made an effort to suppress the tears that were begging to be let loose.

I had no idea what was wrong.

LOOKING INSIDE

I've already named two of my idols, alcohol and a Corvette, but much more important for you is to name your own forms of idolatry. You probably have some ideas already, but delving deeper might be helpful.

Let's start with Timothy Keller's definition of an idol: "Anything more important to you than God, anything that absorbs your heart and imagination more than God, anything you seek to give you what only God can give."[1]

Let me add one more fact before you proceed. As a part of Satan's lie, the temptation to turn to an idol always will be presented to you as seemingly attractive or advantageous. At the same time, its longer-term negative ramifications will not be evident. For example, I initially perceived alcohol to be the solution to all my social problems and ended up with nothing but problems.

With these things in mind, move forward with your self-examination.

When the chips are down, where do you turn?

If not to God, then an idol.

Where do you seek your value and security?

If not from God, then an idol.

Fill in the blank at the end of this sentence: ***"In order to be truly happy, I must ______________________."***[2] If what you placed in the blank does not refer to your relationship with the Lord, you've named an idol.

"If you work very hard at your job and are still passed over for promotion, your response will reveal whether you're serving God or worshiping an idol," according to author Elyse Fitzpatrick.[3]

Wives, if you make a nice dinner for your husband and he ignores you, watches television, and goes to bed and you get angry and cry or pout or look for ways to punish him, you can know that your love for God isn't the predominant love in your life.[4]

Husbands, suppose you've gone the extra mile by taking out the garbage and putting down the toilet seat on two or three recent occasions. Then come bedtime, your wife is "not in the mood." In fact, she turns her back to you and soon starts snoring. If you get angry and cry or pout or look for ways to punish her, you already know what this means.

Single men, are you envious when you look at married couples and imagine that each night for them is the sexual extravaganza that you desire?

Single women, are you envious when you look at married couples and believe their relationship gives them all the security anyone would ever want?

Dan B. Allender and Tremper Longman III offer the following questions for idol identification:

What do you daydream about?

How do you think about your future?

What occupies your thoughts?

What do you spend most of your time doing?

What would you like to spend most of your time doing?

In what ways do you envy others?[5]

Keller admonishes readers in this way: "Look at your most uncontrollable emotions… especially those that never seem to lift and that drive you to do things you know are wrong… When you pull your emotions up by the roots, as it were, you will often find your idols clinging to them."[6]

The author describes how to discover those idols at the roots of your emotions:

> ***If you are angry ask, "Is there something here too important to me, something I must have at all costs?"*** *Do the same thing with strong fear or despair and guilt.* ***Ask yourself, "Am I so scared, because something in my life is being threatened that I think is a necessity when it is not? Am I so down on myself because I have lost or failed at something that I think is a necessity when it is not?"*** *If you are overworking, driving yourself into the ground with frantic activity, ask yourself,* ***"Do I feel that I must have this thing to be fulfilled and significant?"[7]***

Keller also differentiates between what he terms as "surface idols" that are "visible and concrete"[8] like money in comparison to "deep idols," such as "power, approval, comfort, or control."[9] According to the author, the surface idols are things "through which our deep idols seek fulfillment."[10]

In this way, according to Keller, "a surface idol may serve to generate a different set of fears and a different set of hopes."[11]

He gave this example:

> *Money can be a surface idol that serves to satisfy more foundational impulses. Some people want lots of money as a way to control their world and life. Such people usually don't spend much money and live very modestly... Others want money for access to social circles and make themselves beautiful and attractive. These people do spend their money on themselves in very lavish ways. Other people want money because it gives them so much power over others. In every case, money functions as an idol and yet, because of various deep idols, it results in very different patterns of behavior.*[12]

Finally, taking it down to the bare essentials, Fitzpatrick wrote,

> *(Are you) willing to sin to obtain your goal or if you sin when you don't get what you want, then your desire has taken God's place and you're functioning as an idolater?*[13]

WHAT NO CAR COULD DO

Why did I feel like crying after purchasing the car I'd dreamed of owning most of my life? It had nothing to do with the car itself but rather was an indicator that something was spiritually wrong with me.

Sitting inside that sports car, I was not transformed instantaneously into a new and improved Don who was loved by women and both admired and envied by men. I did not feel on the inside as good as the other guys driving Corvettes looked on the outside. I was treated no differently by friends and others than the previous day when I was driving a rusty 1964 Pontiac Tempest.

I harbored unrealistic expectations that possessing this automobile would do for me what I could not do for myself—things I now know only God can do. (Ditto for my alcoholism.)

That's why I wanted to cry.

The Corvette was a surface idol serving as a façade for deeper idols having to do with value and security.

"One of the worst things God can do to someone is to give 'them over in the sinful desires of their hearts,'" wrote Keller while quoting Paul from Romans 1:24.

He elaborates:

> *Why would the greatest punishment imaginable be to allow someone to achieve their fondest dreams? It is because our hearts fashion these desires into idols… If we look to some created thing to give us the meaning, hope, and happiness that only God himself can give, it will eventually fail to deliver and break our hearts.*[14]

That accounts for the emptiness and sadness. I was trying to put a 1963 Corvette into the hole in my heart that only God could fill.

Looking to my past, I can see that pornography became an idol during adolescence. Though I had put on Christ in baptism at age 11 and planned to serve God my entire life, lust served as my gateway drug to alcoholism by desensitizing me to God's will. By the time I became a regular beer drinker my senior year of high school, I didn't care whether drunkenness was a sin.

With so many seeming upsides to drinking, I threw myself headlong into serving the idol of alcohol. This led in college and beyond to worshipping at the altar of "if it feels good, do it" as a part of the arrogance-of-youth movement in the late 1960s.

Besides sex, booze, and the aforementioned Corvette, some of my other idols have been perfectionism, people pleasing, resentments, food, golf, fishing, exercising, the next college degree, completion of the next book, the next girlfriend (until I finally got married at age 55), managing my time and my work as it applied to both teaching and writing.

I've been aware of these idols for a long time and have repented of them, yet some of them occasionally surface today. (Golf is no longer a problem because my perfectionism forced me to quit playing it.) Okay, all of them are still problems except for golf and the next girlfriend.

Hopefully, you've gained some insight into your own idolatry. In the following chapters, you may become aware of some idols that you haven't identified yet as such.

C H A P T E R   F I V E

Idols in Hiding

Cubs, bears, grizzlies, lions, tigers, bobcats, panthers, coyotes, and penguins.

Besides the fact that they are all animals that may be found at a zoo, what do the above creatures have in common?

One answer is that they are the mascots for professional athletic teams playing at the highest levels of the four major sports in the U.S. —football, baseball, basketball, and hockey. A complete listing of such mascots includes many mammals, birds, and fish, plus a snake (diamondbacks) and insect (hornets). If you go into the college ranks, there are many other living things serving as mascots, including a shell-less mollusk (The University of California-Santa Cruz Banana Slugs).

The people who play for these teams (except perhaps for the Banana Slugs) are referred to as sports idols. Their followers are fans, a shortened version of the word *fanatics*.

In terms of devotion to the Egyptian sacred cows, frogs, crocodiles, etc., how do U.S. sports fans compare in devotion to their teams represented by a myriad of animals?

Christian author Mark Driscoll addressed this issue:

> *When our culture is considered through the lens of worship and idolatry, primitive ancient paganism seems far less primitive or ancient. This is because everyone everywhere is continually worshiping, and idolatry is, sadly, seen more easily when we examine other cultures rather than our own.*[1]

So if we think the Egyptian myth about the circumstances leading up to Isis giving birth to Horus is nutty, how might the idols of our culture be viewed by a Christian society living in isolation on a remote Pacific island for the past century?

HIDDEN IDOLS

The concept of culture is all-encompassing because it is "a way of life of a group of people—the behaviors, beliefs, values, and symbols that they accept, generally without thinking about them, and that are passed along from one generation to the next."[2]

In other words, starting from birth, we're surrounded by our culture, and it becomes a part of who we are.

Since culture is so pervasive, the notion of being too close to the forest to see the trees works against anyone in recognizing the effects of their own culture on themselves.

Author Edward Hall said it this way, "Culture hides much more than it reveals, and strangely enough what it hides, it hides most effectively from its own participants."[3]

Others use the following metaphor to explain the same phenomenon: "Cultural values and influences are the ocean in which we all swim and, of which, most of us are completely unaware."[4]

As an example, some Christian missionaries from the U.S. ministering in Russia were told: "Besides teaching us to become Christians, you are also trying to teach us to be Americans." The missionaries had no idea the extent to which their U.S. culture was a part of their religion.

What about us? There are undoubtedly many things we more or less view as universal truths that are true only in our own culture, and in this way, our idols may be hidden from us.

Volumes could be written on how Christians may unwittingly be influenced negatively by their culture. To show some possibilities, I have provided below three broad examples of the changing tide of our culture. Soul-searching and prayerful consideration may help you to discover some idols that have been previously hidden from you.

1. LET ME ENTERTAIN YOU

Looking at an online version of *The Detroit Free Press* this morning, I saw a headline on the sports page about a Detroit Lions football player who had signed a $10 million contract. I didn't blink at the amount because professional athletes regularly sign multi-year deals for tens, even hundreds of millions of dollars.

It is understood that any major league sports player earns much more money than a teacher, a factory worker, or in most cases, your family doctor. Right?

But it hasn't always been like this.

While growing up in Michigan, one of my favorite baseball players for the Detroit Tigers was Frank Lary, known as "The Yankee Killer" because of his uncanny success against the New

York Yankees. Lary pitched for the Tigers from 1954 to 1964. One time, I heard how much money he was making; it was about 50% more than my dad's salary as the foreman at a wholesale meat company.

Another player for the Tigers of particular interest to me was Harry Chiti, a second-string catcher traded to Detroit in the early 1960s. Chiti moved to Farmington, and his daughter was a student in the kindergarten class taught by my mother at Ten Mile Elementary School. If someone wanted to meet Chiti in the off-season, he was easy enough to find working in the produce department of a nearby grocery store.

These days, there are no expectations that athletes at the highest professional levels will work at off-season jobs. Further, unlike earlier, there is a huge gap between an average wage earner and these same pro athletes.

I've put together some numbers below to demonstrate a possible cultural idol that many people may not recognize as such and how its status has grown within past decades.

Available on the internet were median (mid-point) U.S. household incomes from the U.S. Census Bureau and mean (average) baseball salaries available from Major League Baseball, allowing me to contrast the two across a period of years.

With the most recent salary year available (2010), I used 1975 as a comparison because it was the year before the advent of free agency in professional baseball. Prior to free agency, players were the "property" of the team that signed them and could negotiate only with the owners of the team for which they played. Starting in 1976, players were allowed at certain points of their careers to sign with the team that bid the most money for them. In other words, market conditions started to apply.

Here are the numbers:

Comparison of Average Major League Baseball Salaries to Median U.S. Household Incomes

	1975	2010	X's Greater
Median HH income	$13,719	$50,221	3.7
Mean MLB salary	$44,676	$3,014,572	67.5
X's Greater	3.3	60.0	

Reading across, household incomes were 3.7 times higher from 1975 to 2010 while Major League Baseball salaries were 67.5 times greater during the same time period. Reading down, the average salary of a Major League Baseball player was 3.3 times greater than the median household salary in 1975 compared to 60.0 times greater in 2010.

What accounts for this growing gap between family incomes compared to those of professional athletes? Some people mention greed of the players, the owners, or both. These accusations may or may not be true, but it really boils down to what our society thinks is important.

It is, after all, the general public that foots the bill for those multi-million dollar salaries. High ratings for sporting events on television and radio convert to more advertising dollars which go to the media and the teams. This is not to mention money spent on game attendance, concessions, and team paraphernalia.

We could find about the same story in comparisons of salaries with the top tier of other professional sports.

The phenomenon also extends into the college football ranks when the salaries of coaches are compared. For example, Bo Schembechler's salary as head football coach of the University of Michigan was $60,000 in 1969.[5] In 2010, Nick Saban, head football coach at the University of Alabama, was the highest paid college coach making over $6 million. He was followed by Mack Brown at the University of Texas at $5.1 million.[6]

Jesus said, "Where your treasure is, there your heart will be also" (Matthew 6:21). This begs the question for each of us as to where we are investing our treasures.

Earlier quoted was Bruce Feiler who wrote that the ancient Egyptians "worshiped the sun, because it's powerful" and "worshiped the crocodile, because it was strong."[7] Are our reasons for idolizing professional athletes so much different? Were my reasons for idolizing a Corvette any different?

The Egyptians also worshiped the water of the Nile because it gave them irrigation. What do professional athletes give us? Entertainment all day, every day available on any number of cable sports channels and sports-talk formats on radio.

In addition to professional athletes, our treasure goes to many other types of entertainment, including television, movies, concerts, DVDs, CDs, electronic games—the list goes on.

In terms of time and money spent plus overall loyalty, is there a form of entertainment that supersedes your devotion to God?

2. THE SEXUAL REVOLUTION

In his well-documented article on the downward slide of

sexual mores, Dr. John R. Diggs quoted this African proverb: "Don't tear down a fence until you know why it was put up." He elaborates on this parable in the two paragraphs below.

> *The societal implications of the unrestrained sexual activity (which the author had described) are devastating. The ideal of sexual activity being limited to marriage, always defined as male-female, has been a fence erected in all civilizations around the globe. Throughout history, many people have climbed over the fence, engaging in premarital, extramarital and homosexual sex. Still, the fence stands; the limits are visible to all. Climbing over the fence, metaphorically, has always been recognized as a breach of those limits, even by the breachers themselves. No civilization can retain its vitality for multiple generations after removing the fence.*
>
> *But now social activists are saying that there should be no fence, and that to destroy the fence is an act of liberation. If the fence is torn down, there is no visible boundary to sexual expression. If gay sex is socially acceptable, what logical reason can there be to deny social acceptance of adultery, polygamy, or pedophilia? The polygamist movement already has support from some of the advocates for GLB (gay-lesbian-bisexual) rights. And some in the psychological profession are floating the idea that maybe pedophilia is not so damaging to children after all.*[8]

Have you considered this fence and the movement to demolish it?

The first time I recall wondering about its being breached was when I saw the movie *Goldfinger*, a James Bond thriller, around the time I graduated from high school.

Of course, I knew then that people engaged in pre-marital sex. A few of my friends had done so and told me about it. But in my mind, their sexual activities probably would have been frowned upon by mature adults and society in general.

In *Goldfinger*, the sexual activities of James Bond (portrayed by Sean Connery) made him the 1964 equivalent of the Old West gunfighter with the fastest draw. In that parlance, he had a host of notches on the grip of his pistol that demonstrated his previous victories and was aiming for more.

What caught me by surprise was that the guy wearing the white hat had jumped the fence and the seemingly mature adults who made the movie were in on it. As a teen about to enter college, I wondered what this meant as to the truth in regard to sexual behavior. At the time, I still harbored thoughts that going "all the way" was something to save for marriage.

In earlier movies, there had been plenty of references to sex. But unlike James Bond, the good guys had been upholders of high moral standards.

Romantic comedies from that more innocent time period depicted Doris Day as the "good girl" saving herself for marriage. Rock Hudson, who often played her romantic interest, may have strayed, but by marrying Doris at the end of the movie, he was coming around to a right way of thinking. (Of course, it was discovered later that screen roles of actors may be distantly removed from their off-screen lives.)

"Where the Boys Are," released in 1960, depicted college students on spring break in Fort Lauderdale, Florida. The focus of the story is pre-marital sex—basically, do you or don't you. There was a positive outcome for the young woman who was tempted to have pre-marital sex but didn't and tragedy for the one who did. This was a morality tale for young baby boomers such as myself.

Reflecting changes in sexual attitudes that had occurred in the 24 years that followed was the pitiful remake *Where the Boys Are '84*. Here's how it is described: "Four college girls (three horny, one virginal) ... descend on Fort Lauderdale, Florida in search of cheap sex."[9]

In movies and television programs today, it is common for protagonists to have sexual intercourse with someone they just met, and these characters may be a man and a woman or any other combination. In these "happy scenarios," there are no unwanted pregnancies, sexually transmitted diseases, or other negative consequences.

Short of casual sex, media portrayals assume that people will live together prior to marriage. In the romantic comedy, *You've Got Mail*, for example, the characters portrayed by both Tom Hanks and Meg Ryan each lived with other people while exploring a relationship with each other anonymously via e-mails. In the end, those live-in relationships fell apart, and the leading characters are portrayed as finding true love with each other.

Having studied and researched media effects extensively in my academic career, I see the media as reflecting—not creating—our cultural values. In other words, sexual permissiveness was escalating and becoming more acceptable to a greater number of people, and this is why the James Bond movie hero was depicted as an unabashed fornicator.

As to my personal behavior, the movie *Goldfinger* raised questions as to what was right and wrong but did not prompt me to do the wrong thing while in college. I did the wrong thing because (1) most of my friends at the state university I attended were sexually active and very vocal about their experiences and (2) worshipping the god, alcohol, made it much easier for me to set aside my conscience.

The so-called sexual revolution of the 1960s replaced biblical truths with "if it feels good, do it." Some scholars trace the roots of that movement to the mid-1940s when "societal views of the role of sex began changing from a predominantly procreative activity to one focused on individual satisfaction and self-expression."[10]

Of course, the revolution went into full bloom when I was in college and has played a huge role in spawning our now sex-obsessed society.

With few existing taboos when it comes to sex between "consenting adults," there have been numerous problems on both an individual and societal level. The world's "solution" to these problems is a cry for more education and "safe sex," which is really not safe at all. In the face of these measures, problems compound, but the so-called solution remains the same—even more education and supposedly safer sex.

Our culture has done a 180-degree turn in defining the "bad guys." Now, according to our culture, you are the villain wearing the black hat if you are so intolerant as to believe that any sexual act between consenting adults outside of marriage is wrong.

It is not credible to believe that we can live in a sex-drenched culture and not have it affect us. There are numerous statistics indicating the rampant use of internet pornography among Christian men and women, ministers not excluded.

On what side of the fence do you reside?

Do you justify things in your life you know are wrong?

Can you really say you are unaffected by the sexual attitudes of our culture?

3. A GODLESS CULTURE

How did we arrive at a place where you are the intolerant bad guy for believing there is anything wrong with sex between two men, two women, or an unmarried man and woman? The answer involves changes in world views as to what constitutes the truth that are traced briefly below.

Bible-believing Christians subscribe to a world view known as ethical theism, whereby "right and wrong are absolute, unchanging, and they are decided (and communicated to men and women) by God," wrote authors Josh McDowell and Bob Hostetler.[11] This world view has provided the foundation of truth and morality for Western Civilization, including the writing of the U.S. Constitution, according to the authors.

Chipping away at ethical theism over a period of several centuries is a perspective known as modernism, which elevates man and his accomplishments over those of God. This world view often is traced to the so-called Enlightenment period starting in the 1600s where philosophers such as Voltaire and Descartes "claimed that if there was a God who had created the world, he had no contact with it now."[12]

The creation story for modernism became Charles Darwin's theory of evolution. In the early decades following its introduction in 1859, many of our ancestors probably laughed at Darwin's ideas. Not so today, though. For example, at Southern Methodist University in Dallas, Texas, where I served on the faculty for 22 years, a large number of evolutionist faculty members tried to prevent a creationist seminar from being held on campus. What happened to ideas about free speech these same people would be so quick to espouse on so many other issues?

According to Don Closson, modernism "rejects the authority of the church or religion in general and replaces it with the power of individual minds utilizing the methodology of science."[13] From there, it is assumed that if people keep adding to their volumes of knowledge via scientific research, they will be able to solve all human problems and create an earthly utopia.

> *Modernism tells a story of mankind as its own savior that is, with the help of science; modernism has no need for a savior provided by God. Sin is not in its vocabulary, and redemption is not needed; humans lack only education...*
> according to Closson.[14]

> *In the eyes of modernists, any truth that could not be observed or experienced—such as spiritual or moral truth—was relative (that is, different from person to person)...*
> wrote McDowell and Hostetler.[15]

This led to a point where Paul C. Vitz, a long-time professor of psychology, observed,

> *The universities are so deeply secularized that most academics can no longer articulate why they are opposed to Christianity. They merely assume that for all rational people the question of being a Christian was settled—negatively—at some time in the past.*[16]

Before proceeding, it is important to observe that our society enjoys numerous advantages due to scientific advancements, and there is no conflict between a world view of ethical theism and science. In fact, as observed by Eric L. Johnson, "Throughout the history of Christianity, science has been seen, fundamentally, as a gift of God."[17] The conflict arises with modernist views that exclude God and elevate humanity to gods.

Following modernism, the next step was post-modern thought, believed to have become a "cultural phenomenon" between 1960 and 1990 which takes modernism a step further.[18] According to this perspective, truth exists only "in the eye of the beholder. Truth is what is true for you, but there is no such thing as *the* truth," according to author Gene Edward Veith, Jr.[19]

Through the post-modern eye,

> *Any system or statement that claims to be objectively true or unfavorably judges the values, beliefs, lifestyle, and truth claims of another culture is a power play, an effort by one culture to dominate other cultures.*[20]

Christians then became the intolerant ones guilty of judging if, for instance, they use the Bible as the source of truth to establish sexual standards. Someone adhering to a post-modern view would say, "How dare you judge me by your standards." The Christian response would be, "I'm not judging you by my standards, but simply saying you are wrong by God's standards." In most cases, this would be mocked or fall on deaf ears.

If each person is in charge of creating his or her own truth, that means each person is his/her own god. Ultimately, such thinking leads to chaos, and this is exactly what we expect because when people become gods unto themselves, they are being led by Satan.

The biblical statement, "People did whatever they felt like doing" (Judges 21:25, *The Message*) describes rampant idolatry and moral depravity. It also could describe the effects of post-modernism.

Veith cited a poll showing the post-modern influence on Christians. In it, 53% of individuals professing to be Christian did not believe in absolute truth.[21]

In what ways have you subscribed to a modern or post-modern mindset?

To what extent have you been misled by modernist beliefs that science ultimately will solve man's problems?

In what way is God's truth relative or not relative?

How much have you bought into the post-modern lie that you are guilty of judging by calling something a sin when it is defined that way in the Bible?

Seven Similarities Between the Culture of Ancient Egypt and Our Own

1. Idolatry was/is rampant in both.
2. People worship idols that are powerful and that have the ability to give them seemingly positive payouts.
3. The children of Israel probably did not know the extent to which they were influenced by Egypt's godless culture, the very same as our idols are masked to us by our own culture.
4. As were the children of Israel, we are accustomed to living in a land of slavery. This is what we know best, and our very identities are impacted by the idols we worship.
5. The children of Israel were straddling a fence, theologically speaking, and were not comfortable as slaves. We, too, worship both God and gods. Because of this, we often are not comfortable in our own skins. We yearn for something better but have a hard time identifying what really ails us.
6. The myth that led Egyptian Pharaohs to believe they were God is silly and without basis in reality. If we were to write down our ideas about how our false gods came together, they, too, would sound silly.
7. God wanted to lead the children of Israel out of slavery. He wants the same for us.

CHAPTER SIX

A Powerful Demonstration

If you've made the decision to leave the land of slavery and announce your intentions, don't anticipate a going-away party. In fact, you may expect fully that forces both within and without will work toward keeping you footed firmly in bondage.

That's the way it worked for the children of Israel. That's the way it worked for me.

After leaving the mental hospital and not drinking, I had the desire to change my life but was stark raving sober. I had used alcohol as a means of dealing with anxieties and irrational fears, but these problems did not disappear immediately as a result of attending recovery meetings and returning to church. (Besides, you already know that I continued with some old, self-destructive behaviors.)

Sometimes I would go several days in a row with inner shakes, a feeling that there were a thousand moths lost inside my body trying to find a way out. At other times, anxieties and a fear of impending doom seemed like they would overpower me.

There were also intermittent feelings of rage, and just about any small thing could set me off. I remember cursing loudly in my car because I had to stop at a red light.

Sometimes, I had nightmares of drinking alcohol and would get up the next morning feeling like I had a hangover, including a dry-as-a-desert mouth that persisted throughout the day. After awakening from such a dream, it sometimes took several hours for me to realize it hadn't happened in reality.

During those years of heavy drinking, I had no idea that my body was saturated with sugar from beer and booze. As a result, I turned down offers of dessert after a meal and generally spurned sweets. That all changed. One afternoon after I'd been sober for a month or so, I drove to the corner store and bought a six-pack of Yoo-Hoo Chocolate Drink. I had no idea that one bottle contained 23 grams of sugar.

Returning to my apartment, I put five Yoo-Hoos in the refrigerator and kept out one to drink. I took some long swigs from the bottle and quickly downed the whole thing. Disappointed that it had disappeared so quickly and still wanting more, I took out a second bottle and chugged it. I then removed a third bottle... To cut to the chase, I guzzled the entire six-pack in about five minutes.

Even then, I recognized this as blatant compulsivity.

The most pressing of my problems was a phobia of driving in my car. A few years earlier, I'd had anxiety attacks while driving. I discovered that a dose of alcohol would temporarily take away the unease that led to such an attack. Of course, in the long term, alcohol only made the driving anxieties worse. It got to the point where I became terrified of leaving my apartment and driving even a mile or two without prior "fortification."

I was consistently guilty of drinking and driving and usually stashed the empty cans beneath my car seat. It got to the point where the empties would roll out every time I hit the brakes. Then I had to kick them back under.

I finally got around to removing them one day and was curious as to the number that had accumulated. I counted 43. There was also something under there that astounded me—an empty soft-drink can. How it got there, I'll never know because I never touched the stuff.

Once sober, I had to face the driving phobia without turning to my long-time idol. It was not easy. Sometimes before getting in the car to drive, my heart would race, and I'd find myself trembling. Rather than allowing this to serve as a deterrent to even leave my apartment as it had earlier, I forced myself to move forward anyway.

MOSES BLAMED

The children of Israel also ran into plenty of problems in their attempt to leave the land of slavery.

After they called out for help, Moses and Aaron appeared with God's message of deliverance. Moses performed miraculous signs, and the people believed. "And when they heard that the Lord was concerned about them and had seen their misery, they bowed down and worshipped" (Exodus 4:31).

After that, things grew worse.

We saw earlier that Pharaoh refused the entreaty of Moses and Aaron to let the Hebrews go worship God in the desert.

Pharaoh then asked Moses and Aaron, "Why are you taking the people away from their labor? Get back to your work! Look, the people of the land are now numerous, and you are stopping them from working" (Exodus 5:4-5).

Later that day, Pharaoh talked to his slave-drivers about the Israelites. "They are lazy. That is why they are crying out, 'Let us go and sacrifice to our God.' Make the work harder for the men so that they keep working and pay no attention to lies" (Exodus 5:8-9).

To accomplish his purpose, Pharaoh gave the order to stop supplying straw to the Hebrew slaves making bricks. This meant they would have to scour the country to find stubble for straw while producing the same quota of bricks as previously. When they failed to meet that quota, the Hebrew foremen overseeing the brick-making were abused physically.

The children of Israel blamed Moses and Aaron and told them about it. "May the Lord look upon you and judge you! You have made us a stench to Pharaoh and his officials and have put a sword in their hand to kill us" (Exodus 5:20).

Contrast this to the welcome Moses and Aaron had received from the children of Israel just shortly before. As it turned out, the theory of leaving the land of slavery was much easier than the reality of actually doing it.

When things got tough—and there is no doubt that they did, the Israelites suddenly were more concerned about pleasing their ultimate slave-master, Pharaoh, than the Lord God who wanted to free them. Their very identities were based on the lies of their culture that they deserved nothing better than slavery and that they ultimately answered to the Egyptian god of gods.

When Moses subsequently tried to talk to them about God's deliverance, "They did not listen to him because of their discouragement and cruel bondage" (Exodus 6:9).

In what way have you discovered that things grow more difficult as you've tried to abandon the idols that have kept you in slavery?

LOUDER THAN WORDS

Rather than having Moses go back to them with more words, God apparently decided to show the Israelites that he had both the strength to deliver them and the desire to do so. This was accomplished through a series of plagues that devastated the Egyptians but not the Israelites.

According to the biblical text, the purpose of the 10 plagues was to convince Pharaoh (Exodus 4:21-23; 6:1), the Israelites (Exodus 6:7; 8:22; 10:1-2), and the Egyptians (Exodus 7:5; 14:4,18) that the Lord is God. Undoubtedly, God's work in the plagues also was preserved in written form to serve as testimony to us.

Each plague unmasked the powerlessness of one or more of the Egyptian gods and goddesses. (For a listing of Egyptian gods debunked during the plagues, see the display "Egyptian Deities Brought Under God's Judgment During the Plagues.")

John J. Davis observed, "The plagues served to demonstrate the impotency of Pharaoh, both as a ruler and as a god. He was subject to the same frustrations and anxieties as the average man in Egypt during the period of the plagues."[1]

"It was appropriate," wrote Davis, "that the first of the plagues should be directed against the Nile River itself, the very lifeline of Egypt and the center of many of its religious ideas."[2]

While the river reached its lowest ebb each May, monsoon rains and melting snow from the mountains of Ethiopia caused the Nile to start rising in June. The river peaked with flooding during September, providing a thick layer of highly fertile silt in the Nile valley.[3]

Egyptian agriculture was dependent on the Nile's annual overflow which provided marshland for the grazing of livestock and irrigation and added deposits of lush soil for crops.

In some years, the inundation of water was not high enough

Egyptian Deities Brought Under God's Judgment During the Plagues[8]

Nile Turned to Blood, Exodus 7:14-24. The Nile was thought to be the bloodstream of the god, Osiris. The god who caused the Nile to overflow its banks was Hapy, Hapi, or Hopi, known as "the spirit of the Nile." He was depicted as an obese man with woman-like breasts and skin that was colored either blue or

green. Other deities believed to be directly involved with the Nile were Khnum, guardian of the river, who had the body of a man and the head of a long-horned ram; Neith, a goddess who took a special interest in crocodiles and

Khnum

to reach all of the farmlands. In other years, it was so high that it swept away homes and killed people. "The whole welfare of the country depended on this one phenomenon, and because of this the ancient Egyptians seemed to have felt uniquely blessed and uniquely vulnerable," wrote Geraldine Pinch.[4]

The Nile also was a source of fish to eat, served as the principle mode of transportation between northern and southern Egypt, and by virtue of emptying into the Mediterranean Sea, provided a means of commerce with the rest of the known world.

Not only did the Nile turn to blood as a part of the first plague, so did the water in streams, canals, reservoirs, and even water stored in buckets and jars (Exodus 7:19). This resulted in an

Nile perch; and her son, Sobek, the chief crocodile god. Neith was pictured as nursing crocodiles and her son was depicted as either a crocodile or a man with a crocodile head.

Frogs, Exodus 8:1-15. Married to Khnum named earlier, Heqt or Heket appeared as a frog or with the head of a frog. She was associated with the resurrection of the dead, childbirth, and fertility. This latter characteristic was extended beyond human fertility to agricultural applications. The sound of croaking frogs were an indication that the gods of the Nile had once again made the land fertile. Thus, the frogs were considered sacred and represented

immediate change in lifestyle; everyone had to dig along the banks of the Nile for drinking water (Exodus 7:24).

Davis wrote, "One can well imagine the horror and frustration of the people of Egypt as they looked upon that which was formerly beautiful only to find dead fish lining the shores and an ugly red characterizing what had before provided life and attraction."[5] And this is not to mention the stench emanating from the river (Exodus (7:18).

With each passing plague, the misery of Egypt grew to new heights, finally culminating in the 10th and final plague, death of the first-born of both Egyptian people and cattle. This resulted in "loud wailing in Egypt, for there was not a house without someone

"fruitfulness, blessing and the assurance of a harvest."[9] Frogs are depicted in Egyptian art work and in the form of amulets. A frog could not be killed, even by accident.

Dust Turned into Gnats, Exodus 8:16-19. Some versions of the Bible refer to these insects as lice or sand fleas. As god of the earth, Geb was the overseer of dust. Geb was portrayed as a man, sometimes with green skin. This plague hit both man and animals, which also would include those viewed as being sacred. Experts believe that priests were the hardest hit by this plague because the uncleanness of the bug bites made them unfit to perform their priestly duties.

Flies/Swarms, Exodus 8:20-32. The Hebrew word translated as "flies" may mean a wide variety of insects, "swarms," drawn to the decaying frogs to lay their eggs. Anubis is one candidate for dead" (Exodus 12:30).

"The death cry which was heard throughout Egypt was not only a wail that bemoaned the loss of a son or sacred animals, but also the incapability of the many gods of Egypt to respond and protect them from such tragedy," wrote Davis.[6]

The plagues must have shaken the foundations of Egyptian assumptions regarding what constituted truth.

GOD'S POWER TODAY

The Lord can do the same things with our idols.

Do you really believe this?

There seem to be many Christian people who recognize their

an Egyptian god associated with this plague. He had the body of man and the head of jackal or wild dog and was associated with bandaging and embalming mummies. Some sources associate this plague with Khepri, who appeared in artwork with the head of a scarab beetle and the body of either a man or a hawk. Like flies, scarab beetles are attracted to dung as a place to leave their eggs.

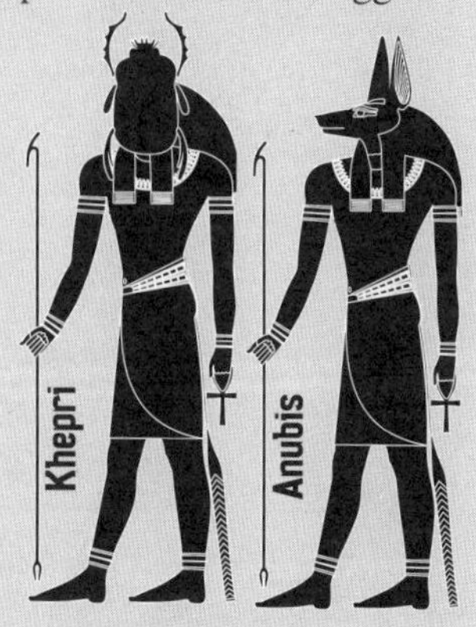

Death of Cattle and Livestock, Exodus 9:1-7. Cows were treated as sacred animals. Bulls were associated with strength and virility, and Pharaoh was viewed as the strongest bull. An actual bull was selected to be the Apis bull, the most sacred animal in Egypt. When an Apis bull died, it idolatry and believe they can be forgiven. Their mindset, however, often does not include a belief that God can defeat their idols.

J. B. Phillips addressed this point in his book, *Your God is Too Small*, which is well worth reading.

"The trouble with many people today is that they have not found a God big enough for modern needs," writes Phillips. "While their experience of life has grown in a score of directions, and their mental horizons have been expanded to the point of bewilderment by world events and scientific discoveries, their ideas of God have remained largely static."[7]

There are also self-reliant Christians who subscribe to cultural messages such as, "You can do anything you set your mind to;"

was mummified, and then its successor was selected on the basis of a number of physical markings. This bull was associated with the god, Ptah, who was believed to have created the world with his heart and tongue. He was pictured as a bearded man with blue skin and wearing a shroud. Heifers were considered sacred to Isis. Also connected to cattle was Hathor, the mother goddess who provided love and protection. She was depicted in various ways,

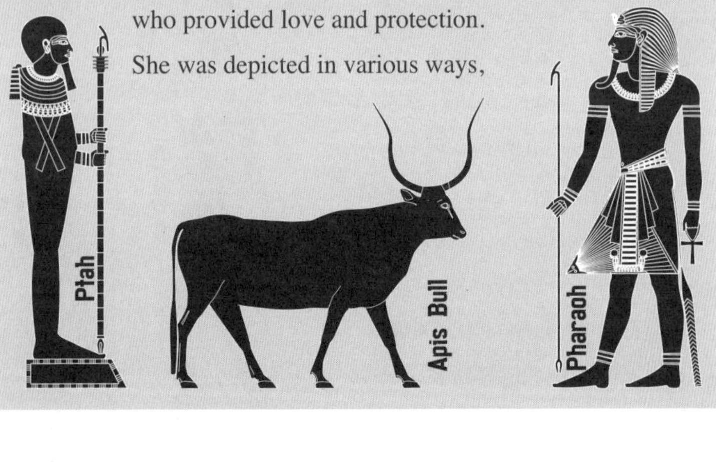

"You can pull yourself up by your own bootstraps;" "You can accomplish anything if you work hard enough."

Such ideas fly in the face of Paul's statement, "I can do everything through him who gives me strength" (Philippians 4:13). Ultimately, then, it is the Lord who will eradicate our idols—not us.

How has your self-reliance trumped out reliance in God in your daily life?

In terms of my own anxieties and fears during those early months of sobriety, it seemed as if I would take three steps forward, one backward, two forward, three backward. Sometimes, I was discouraged greatly by the ongoing setbacks. However, I continued going to both the recovery meetings and church and took

including as a cow nursing a king, a woman with a cow's head, and a woman with the horns of a cow.

Boils and Sores, Exodus 9:8-12. The boils and sores affected both men and animals. Imhotep, an actual person who lived around 2700 B.C., was deified after his death and became known as the god of knowledge and healing. He was said to have been a son of Ptah. Sekhamet, a lion-headed goddess, was the patron goddess of medicine. She had the power to both initiate epidemics and bring them to an end. As the god of wisdom and secret knowledge, Thoth would have access to medical learning.

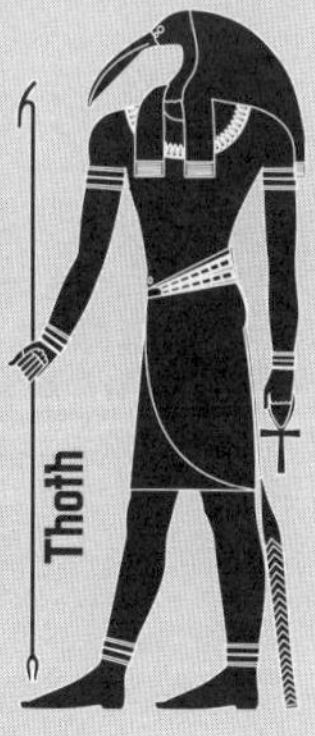

home messages from each. While trying to grow in faith, I learned three things I could count on during those difficult times:

1. THIS TOO SHALL PASS.

I applied this to anxieties and depression that dogged me during the early years of my sobriety. Previous to this, I always assumed that things would always grow continually worse until I went crazy. Come to find out, those down times always proved to be temporary and in the long run, all but disappeared.

2. A DRINK WILL NOT MAKE IT ANY BETTER.

Returning to the old idol never will help. For years, I had

He was pictured as either a baboon or a man with an ibis head.

Hail, Thunder and Lightning, Exodus 9:13-35. Nut was the sky goddess. Depicted as either a huge naked woman or a cow, Nut was powerless to prevent this destruction of crops. She was the mother of Isis, Osiris, and Set. Also, see the Egyptian deities named later in regard to the locust plague.

Locusts, Exodus 10:1-20. Isis and Set each had responsibilities regarding remaining crops which were destroyed by the locusts. Isis was worshipped widely and known as creating

medicated myself with liquor during bad times, but these self-prescriptions had diminishing effects and finally led me to despair.

3. GOD WILL NEVER GIVE YOU ANY MORE THAN YOU CAN HANDLE.

This is based on I Corinthians 10:13, "No temptation has seized you except what is common to man. And God is faithful; he will not let you be tempted beyond what you can bear. But when you are tempted, he will also provide a way out so that you can stand up under it." When the bad times did come, I came to have the confidence that I could stand up under them and didn't need to drink in a vain attempt to fix myself.

agriculture. Her evil brother, Set, was sometimes associated with vineyards and as a protector of crops. Renenutet was linked to all kinds of food, including the healing powers of mother's milk; she sometimes was pictured as a cobra-headed woman nursing a child. Her daughter, Neper or Nepri, was the goddess of grain, specifically corn.

Darkness, Exodus 10:21-29. Ra or Re, the sun god, "was the ultimate source of light, energy, and life"[10] and the most worshipped Egyptian deity, except Pharaoh. Pharaohs referred to themselves as sons of Ra. Also associated with the sun was Khepri, who was in charge of the dawn that transformed darkness to light. Khepri was also mentioned earlier in relation to flies/swarms and

Ra

I also looked around at the recovery meetings. Good things were happening in the lives of those who stayed sober. Among those who resumed drinking, there was inevitable disaster.

I'm sorry to report that one person who returned to drinking was Ron, the man who carried the message to me in the mental hospital. One day I called over to his house, and his mother answered. She said he was dead drunk. He never called me back and after that, I lost track of him.

In spite of this, I did not lose hope that God is stronger than the idol of alcohol and any other idol you and I may encounter.

In what way have you found this to be true in your own life?

was depicted with the head of a scarab beetle. These beetles rolled dung balls up to 50 times their own weight in the same way that Khepri pushed the sun across the sky. "The Lord showed that He had control over the sun as a witness that the God of Israel had ultimate power over life and death."[11]

Death of First-Born Males and Cattle, Exodus 11:1-12:36.

This plague brought "judgment on all the gods of Egypt" (Exodus 12:12). The god most impacted was Pharaoh himself as the embodiment of Horus. The demise of Pharaoh's son, due a double portion of riches as the first-born, also demonstrated that Pharaoh was powerless even in determining his would-be successor. Literal "sacred cows" also died.

CHAPTER SEVEN

Denial by the Nile

Considering that Pharaoh was brought up in a culture that told him he was God, it was no doubt easy to buy into this lie. For him, there were plenty of seeming upsides in this perspective. When he said jump, everyone in Egypt instantly replied, "How high?"

Anyone can "play God" but very few people have an entire nation that goes along with the idea.

The extent of Pharaoh's power and control was apparently unquestioned until Moses showed up with news of God's supremacy. The refusal of the Egyptian ruler to release the Hebrew slaves set up a God versus god match-up, the outcome a no-brainer from the beginning.

We've seen how the 10 plagues proved that God was more powerful than all of Egypt's false gods, including Pharaoh as Egypt's spiritual leader. We also discussed how God is more powerful than our own idols. Like Pharaoh, though, we may have a hard time in recognizing our idolatry and letting go of it.

Most of us are not in charge of a country and don't have the power to create devastation in the lives of thousands or even millions of people, as did Pharaoh and dictators who have followed. But our skewed spiritual perspective can create plenty of problems for the people around us and in the corner of the world over which we have illusions of control.

When our self-will supersedes God's will and in our idolatry we bow down to god instead of God, we have been deceived by Satan, "the father of lies" (John 8:44). In my life this occurred when I turned to alcohol.

If an individual persists in acting on that lie, as I did, that person begins to lie to him or herself. This is denial. The end of denial comes when a person repents by admitting that an idol has been number one in his/her life and starts seeking God. The person who does not repent and continues in denial follows a Satan-led path toward self-destruction.

Do you understand the role of repentance
in turning from idolatry?
How has repentance been a part of your Christian walk?

As you read below about Pharaoh's denial and
self-destructive course, to what extent do you identify?

As the chief god and king of Egypt, Pharaoh's duties included commanding Egypt's powerful army and seeking the best interests of its people. This included overseeing the country's food supply. (See Genesis 41.)

After Pharaoh forced the additional hardship on his Hebrew slaves of making bricks without straw, Moses was discouraged because his fellow Hebrews blamed him. Moses then received the following forecast from God: "Now you will see what I will do to Pharaoh: Because of my mighty hand he will let them go; because of my mighty hand he will drive them out of his country" (Exodus 6:1).

God's first demonstration of power came at the expense of no one. It occurred during the second visit with Pharaoh by Moses and Aaron. As directed by God, Aaron threw his staff to the floor and it became a snake. However, "the Egyptian magicians also did the same things by their secret arts: Each one threw down his staff and it became a snake" (Exodus 7:11-12). It is not clear whether they did this through black magic or sleight of hand, but for a moment, at least, it appeared there would be a stalemate. Then "Aaron's staff swallowed up their staffs" (Exodus 7:12).

In response, the Egyptian king initiated a pattern that would be oft-repeated. "Pharaoh's heart became hard and he would not listen to them" (Exodus 7:13). This demonstrates an aspect of denial whereby people persist in thinking they are right and are blinded to any evidence to the contrary.

This set the stage for the 10 plagues, each one more devastating than the last. While Nero fiddled when Rome burned, what Pharaoh did was much worse. The effects on the country and how he became Egypt's worst enemy may be seen in the accompanying display, "Steam-Rolling Devastation of Plagues and Pharaoh's Responses."

It is said that the height of insanity is repeating the same behaviors with expectations of different results. Denial leads people to do this, Pharaoh not withstanding. The sad thing for the Egyptian people is that the ongoing plagues were unnecessary. Pharaoh's submission to the rule of God at any stage could have averted the plagues that followed, the very same as our true repentance of idolatry can negate further problems for ourselves.

Here are some outcomes of Pharaoh's denial:

Oblivious to Consequences—With each passing plague, the situation in Egypt grew continually worse, but Pharaoh continued on the same self-destructive path. I did the same thing during my years of drunkenness.

Has your denial ever made you blind to the mounting negative consequences in your own life?

Jail-House or Fox-Hole Prayers—These occur when people seek God during an emergency and forget about Him when it is over. During the second plague (frogs), Pharaoh admitted God's superior power by asking Moses to pray that the Lord would take away the frogs. In subsequent plagues Pharaoh sounded like he'd been to a revival meeting; he asked for prayers on his behalf (flies), admitted that he and his people were wrong (hail), twice said he'd sinned (hail, locusts), and asked for forgiveness (hail). In short, he repented.

Despite all this lip service to God's superiority, Pharaoh's heart hardened and he went back to his old ways as soon as the emergencies created by plagues one through nine had passed.

Have you ever repented and then turned around and did the same thing again? I have.

False Promises—Pharaoh agreed to let the Israelites go worship the Lord during the plague of frogs and subsequently. Then when the emergency subsided, Pharaoh's heart grew hard and he reneged on his word.

Have you gone back on pledges you made during difficult times? I have.

Attempted Negotiations with God—During three of the plagues, Pharaoh agreed to let the Hebrews go worship the Lord, but each time he attempted to add restrictions. These included "you must not go very far" (Exodus 8:28) (flies), only the men could go but not the women and children (locusts), and the people could but couldn't take their animals with them (darkness).

Efforts to bargain with God are another sign that Pharaoh still harbored thoughts that he could have it his way and avert the simple truth that God is sovereign.

Have you ever tried to subvert God's will via attempts at bargaining with Him? I have.

Poor treatment of people--During all of this, Pharaoh seemed oblivious to the fact that his arrogance was leading his country on a course of destruction. The suffering of his people grew continually worse with each passing plague, yet he did not relent nor did he show recognition of the damage he was creating by his arrogance. Egypt's food supplies were ruined, undoubtedly creating hardships for people for years thereafter.

Finally, it was a horrible tragedy that could have been averted—the loss of first-born boys and animals among the Egyptian people--that led Pharaoh to tell the Israelites to leave.

One's relationship with God is tied directly to his/her relationships with people, and vice-versa. These facts are demonstrated in The Ten Commandments and the "Big Two" of Jesus which summarize the Ten,

> *"Love the Lord your God with all your heart and with all your soul and with all of your mind." This is the first and greatest commandment. And the second is like it: "Love your neighbor as yourself." All the Law and the prophets hang on these two commandments (Matthew 22:37-40).*

Pharaoh treated the Israelites as his personal property and demonstrated complete disregard for the welfare of his own people.

Has your arrogance led you to treat people poorly?

Mine has.

SIMILARITIES WITH AN IDOL

Earlier, we showed how idols and little-g gods were all from the same source—Satan. Here we'll let excerpts about idols from Psalm 115 demonstrate the devil's influence on Pharaoh's psyche, which to one degree or another occurs with anyone who persists in denial by playing God. As it turns out, Pharaoh was an idol himself and acted accordingly.

Identify ways that each of the characteristics of an idol listed below have applied to you.

"Their idols are silver and gold, made by the hands of men" (Psalm 115:4). As the god of his culture, Pharaoh was a man-made god. He was heartless or had a hardened heart, just like the idols made of silver and gold.

"They have mouths, but cannot speak" (Psalm 115:5). Pharaoh did have a mouth and could speak in a literal sense, but he had nothing to say except words that fed his own arrogance and led to his subsequent downfall.

"(They have) eyes, but they cannot see" (Psalm 115:5). During the fifth plague, death of livestock among the Egyptians, Pharaoh sent men to see what had happened to livestock belonging to the Hebrews. Acting as Pharaoh's eyes, these men discovered those animals in good health, as had been foretold by Moses. Blinded to the truth, Pharaoh's "heart was unyielding" (Exodus 9:7).

"They have ears, but cannot hear" (Psalm 115:6). Pharaoh's "ear problems" kept him from hearing God's truth or showing any recognition of it. The extent of this "deafness" was further demonstrated when he failed to heed the advice of his long-trusted magicians who said, "This is the finger of God" (Exodus 8:19) during the third plague (gnats).

"(They have) noses, but they cannot smell" (Psalm 115:6). What good was it to have a nose if it didn't stimulate Pharaoh to surrender to God after the stench from the dead fish of the first plague or the stinking piles of dead frogs from the second plague?

"They have hands, but cannot feel" (Psalm 115:7). Pharaoh did have hands and could touch things with them, but he had no feelings for the welfare of either the Hebrew or the Egyptian people.

"(They have) feet, but they cannot walk" (Psalm 115:7). He did have feet, but all the evidence in the world could not persuade him to move from his position of arrogance.

"Those who make them will be like them, and so will all who trust in them" (Psalm 115:8). The Egyptian culture that made Pharaoh a god would also suffer the same fate as he did with the loss of their first-born sons during the 10th plague. What does this say about any culture that turns its back on God and relishes its idols?

LOSS OF FREE WILL

As we have seen, Pharaoh continually hardened his heart to God's power. A big change in the hardening process started with the sixth plague when the Egyptians were stricken with boils. After that, the biblical text is clear in indicating that God hardened Pharaoh's heart. (See Exodus 9:12; 10:1; 10:20; 10:27; 11:10; 14:4; 14:8.) This is tantamount to a loss of free will.

On the surface these theological implications seem bothersome. Seemingly, God takes away this person's choice to repent. That's not the way it works, though.

God gave us free will starting with our earliest ancestors in the Garden of Eden. If a person abuses this by continually choosing gods/idols, he/she finally reaches a point of spiritual blindness. This results in the loss of both the ability to make the right choice and the gift of free will. Finally blinded to God's truth, these people view the world through the eyes of Satan whom they were so intent on serving in the first place.

In short, when an individual continually persists in shouting, "My will be done!" God allows that to happen.

This is consistent with the following New Testament passages:

Their foolish hearts were darkened. Although they claimed to be wise, they became fools and exchanged the glory of the immortal God for images made to look like mortal man and birds and animals and reptiles... God gave them over in the sinful desires of their hearts... He gave them over to a depraved mind to do what ought not be done (Romans 1:21-24, 28).

God sends them a powerful delusion so that they will believe the lie (II Thessalonians 2:11).

Since they refuse to trust truth, they're banished to their chosen world of lies and illusions (II Thessalonians 2:12, The Message).

I'll let the words of Rabbi Yoseph Kahanov sum up Pharaoh's reactions to the plagues. In quoting him, I have respected Jewish tradition in regard to the usage of God's name:

The sages explain that when the mind is clouded by the fog of desire and emotion, it becomes blinded to reality to the extent of utter foolishness and self-destruction. Pharaoh's decisions to continue to defy G-d and reality came from his ego-blinded heart with no rationale entering the process. Though he could see his entire dynasty being destroyed, he could not alter his intransigent ways and allow the Children of Israel to leave. So he plunges ahead making deals and promises to G-d only to renege on them the very moment he catches the slightest respite. He is entirely oblivious as to how increasingly small and foolish he appears with each desperate maneuver.[1]

Despite this self-destructive downhill journey for the Egyptian king, he persisted in his denial. Pharaoh's next move, as detailed in the following chapter, had just the opposite effect from what he intended. It demonstrated God's miraculous saving power and served as a springboard toward the Promised Land for the children of Israel.

Steam-Rolling Devastation of Plagues and Pharaoh's Responses

Blood (Exodus 7:14-24): The water in Egypt turned to blood, including the Nile River, streams, canals, ponds, reservoirs, and water stored in buckets and jars. The Nile smelled horrible from the dead fish. For drinking water, people had to dig along the banks of the river. Fishing for both commercial and personal purposes came to a halt. Boat travel along the Nile undoubtedly had to cease, shutting down commerce. How did the people get water to their livestock or for irrigation? Where did the crocodiles and water snakes go during this time?

Pharaoh's response: *"Pharaoh's heart became hard; he would not listen to Moses and Aaron... Instead, he turned and went into his palace" (Exodus 7:22-23).*

Frogs (Exodus 8:1-15): At the onset of this plague, frogs jumped up on the people and could be found everywhere, even on their beds and in their ovens. Considering the religious significance of frogs, did people feel guilty if they accidentally stepped on one or cooked it in the oven? At the conclusion of the plague, "frogs died in the houses, in the courtyards and in the fields. They were piled into heaps, and the land reeked of them" (Exodus 8:13-14). Imagine the resulting revulsion and confusion from the plague itself and the aftermath, not only from a practical standpoint but also from a religious point of view.

Pharaoh's response: *In the following entreaty to Moses and Aaron, Pharaoh acknowledged the Lord as a power greater than himself: "Pray to the Lord to take the frogs away from me and my people, and I will let your people go to offer sacrifices to the Lord"*

(Exodus 8:8). "But when Pharaoh saw that there was relief, he hardened his heart and would not listen to Moses and Aaron..." (Exodus 8:15).

Gnats (lice, sandflies) (Exodus 8: 16-19): These insects, which affected both people and animals, were described as "a species so small as to be hardly visible to the eye but with a very irritating and painful sting."[2] The Hebrew word *kinnim* used to describe these bugs comes from a root which means "to dig," indicating that they dig under the skin.[3] Imagine everyone in an entire nation being affected simultaneously. To what extent would it impact their quality of life and day-to-day routines?

***Pharaoh's response**: The magicians could not give the appearance of replicating this feat, and acknowledged God as greater than Pharaoh by saying, "'This is the finger of God.' But Pharaoh's heart was hard and he would not listen..." (Exodus 8: 19).*

Flies/Swarms (Exodus 8:20-23): This plague and those that remain did not affect the Israelites (Exodus 8:22). "Dense swarms of flies poured into Pharaoh's palace and into the houses of his officials, and throughout Egypt the land was ruined by flies" (Exodus 8:24). The blood-sucking dogflies so hated by the Egyptian people could cause blindness.[4] John J. Davis observes that the Hebrew word used to describe this plague "speaks of something oppressive or burdensome such as a yoke, famine or mourning...The Hebrew expression was obviously intended to convey the sense of intensity or severity."[5]

***Pharaoh's response**: First, Pharaoh said he would let the people worship God in Egypt. When Moses pointed out that they needed* *to take a three-day journey into the desert, Pharaoh said they could go but not very far. He then added, "Now pray for me" (Exodus 8:28). When the flies left, "Pharaoh hardened his heart and would not let the people go" (Exodus 8:28).*

Plague on livestock (Exodus 9:1-7): The previous plagues included inconvenience, pain and irritation, but this was the first to impact personal property. The plague caused death among "livestock in the field" (Exodus 9:3) belonging to the Egyptians including horses, donkeys, camels, cattle, sheep and goats. The infectious bacterial disease, anthrax, is speculated, but this cannot be said with certainty.[6] Davis wrote that this plague had "grave economic consequences"[7] that impacted sources of land transportation and the milk supply.

Pharaoh's response: *Pharaoh went on a tour to see that the Egyptian livestock died, while the animals belonging to the Israelites were unscathed. "Yet his heart was unyielding and he would not let the people go" (Exodus 9:7).*

Boils (Exodus 9:8-12): "Festering boils broke out on men and animals" (Exodus 9:10) perhaps due to skin anthrax.[8] Egyptian magicians were stricken to the point that they were not able to stand before Pharaoh. The term used to describe the boils reflects "not only severe soreness and irritation, but perhaps open and running sores."[9] This plague started after Moses threw handfuls of soot from a furnace in the sight of Pharaoh. Could this have been a furnace used by the Israelite slaves in brick-making?

Pharaoh's response: *"The Lord hardened Pharaoh's heart and he would not listen to Moses and Aaron" (Exodus 9:12).*

Hail (Exodus 9:13-35): Moses told Pharaoh to expect the worst hail storm in the history of Egypt. Some Egyptians heeded the warning by bringing their slaves and livestock inside; others didn't. "Hail fell and lightning flashed back and forth... Throughout Egypt hail struck everything in the fields—both men and animals; it beat down everything growing in the fields and stripped every tree" (Exodus (9:24-25). The field crops destroyed included flax and barley, indicating that this took place in January or early February.[10] Flax was used to make cloth, while barley could be used as animal fodder or to make either bread or beer. "The wheat and spelt, however, were not destroyed, because they ripen later" (Exodus 9:32). "Spelt is an inferior kind of wheat ordinarily raised in Egypt as an after crop."[11]

Pharaoh's response: *During the plague Pharaoh stated, "This time I have sinned. The Lord is in the right, and I and my people are in the wrong" (Exodus 9:27). But when the storm stopped, Pharaoh "and his officials hardened their hearts" (Exodus 9:34). So, he still wouldn't let the Israelites go to worship God.*

Locusts (Exodus 10:1-20): Young locusts simply have hopping ability, but in adulthood they develop wings giving them the ability to sustain flight for miles. "The locust is perhaps nature's most awesome example of the collective destructive power of a species,"[12] wrote Davis. They were greatly feared. Each day a single locust could devour plant life equaling its own body weight. To demonstrate the possible devastation, a swarm of these insects covering one square mile would contain somewhere between 100 and 200 million of them, and one swarm has been known to cover 400 square miles.[13] Egyptian officials had a change of sentiment from the hardening of their hearts during the previous plague.

After Moses warned of the impending locust infestation, they beseeched Pharaoh, "How long will this man be a snare to us? Let the people go, so that they may worship the Lord their God. Do you not yet realize that Egypt is ruined?" (Exodus 10:7) As a seeming bargaining chip prior to the plague that was unacceptable from the get-go, Pharaoh said he would let the men go worship God in the desert but not the women and children. After that, "Moses and Aaron were driven out of Pharaoh's presence" (Exodus 10:11). The locust attack was unprecedented in the history of Egypt (Exodus 10:14). "They covered all the ground until it was black. They devoured all that was left after the hail—everything growing in the fields and the fruit on the trees. Nothing green remained on tree or plant in all the land of Egypt" (Exodus 10:15).

***Pharaoh's response**: After the swarms of locust settled in Egypt, "Pharaoh quickly summoned Moses and Aaron and said, 'I have sinned against the Lord your God and against you. Now forgive my sin once more and pray to the Lord your God to take this deadly plague away from me'" (Exodus 10:16). Yet after God sent a wind to carry the locusts into the sea, "the Lord hardened Pharaoh's heart, and he would not let the Israelites go" (Exodus 10:20).*

Darkness (Exodus 10:21-29): This was described as "darkness that can be felt..." (Exodus 10:21). Total darkness covered most of Egypt for three days (Exodus 10:22), and the Egyptian people could not see anyone else or leave their homes. "Yet all the Israelites had light in the places where they lived" (Exodus 10:23). "The other plagues brought about the destruction of property, personal discomfort and pain, but this plague brought about the total immobilization of the Egyptians and certainly must have resulted in great fear."[14] "The psychological and religious impact would have had a profound influence on the Egyptians. Darkness was a representation of death, judgment and hopelessness."[15]

***Pharaoh's response**: This time Pharaoh agreed to let Israelite men, women and children go into the desert to worship, but they couldn't take their animals with them. Moses said this was not acceptable. "The Lord hardened Pharaoh's heart" (Exodus 10:27). He told Moses to get out of his sight.*

Death of first-born males (Exodus 11:1-10, 12, 29-30): "At midnight the Lord struck down all the firstborn in Egypt, from the firstborn of Pharaoh, who sat on the throne, to the firstborn of the prisoner who was in the dungeon, and the firstborn of all the livestock as well. Pharaoh and all his officials and all the Egyptians got up during the night, and there was a loud wailing in Egypt, for there was not a house without someone dead" (Exodus 12:29-30). The Israelites were spared the loss of first-born males following God's instructions by putting the blood of a one-year-old male lamb or goat on the sides and tops of their door frames (Exodus 12:3-7). They stayed in their homes and celebrated the first Passover meal (Exodus 12:8-11).

***Pharaoh's response**: "During the night Pharaoh summoned Moses and Aaron and said, 'Up! Leave my people, you and the Israelites! Go, worship the Lord as you have requested. Take your flocks and herds, as you have said, and go. And also bless me'" (Exodus 12:31-32).*

CHAPTER EIGHT

Leaving the Land of Slavery

While Pharaoh and all the Egyptians grieved the loss of their first-born sons and animals, the children of Israel were spared the same fate. Following God's instructions, the Hebrews killed year-old male sheep or goats and roasted them as a part of the first Passover meal. Blood from these slaughtered animals was smeared on the top and sides of the doorframes of their homes.

The Lord had said, "The blood will be a sign for you on the houses where you are; and when I see the blood, I will pass over you. No destructive plague will touch you when I strike Egypt" (Exodus 12:13).

As a result of this 10th plague, Pharaoh finally relented and told the children of Israel to leave. Their Egyptian neighbors also said the same thing: "'For otherwise,' they said, 'We will all die!'" (Exodus 12:33).

The next morning, the children of Israel "marched out boldly in full view of all the Egyptians, who were burying all their first-born, whom the Lord had struck down among them; for the Lord had brought judgment on their gods" (Numbers 33:3-4).

Focus on the last part of that quotation: "...the Lord had brought judgment on their gods." This judgment started when Moses arrived in Egypt and escalated through each of the 10 plagues. It finally concluded the day the children of Israel left that country en masse (also, in a mess).

In this conflict between God and gods, God wins every time.

The message is just as applicable today as it was then. God was superior to the gods of Egypt and is superior to the gods worshipped by us personally and in our culture. The Lord continues to bring judgment on little-*g* gods today—either to our benefit or detriment, the choice is ours. Who or what we worship always determines our outcomes in this life and beyond.

How has the Lord brought judgment on your little-g gods?

Departing from Egypt, the children of Israel were inspired by these words from the lips of Moses: "Always remember this day. This is the day when you came out of Egypt from a house of slavery. God brought you out of here with a powerful hand" (Exodus 13:3, *The Message*).

Where had they been? In slavery.

Who delivered them? God.

How important is it that God's people remember these principles? They are mentioned 145 times in the Old Testament.[1]

In fact, both listings of The Ten Commandments start out with them: "I am the Lord your God, who brought you out of Egypt, out of the land of slavery. You shall have no other gods before me" (Exodus 20:2-3; Deuteronomy 5:6-7).

God initially had introduced himself to Moses and the children of Israel as the God of the Patriarchs (Exodus 3:6,15). Now after the Passover, it was God's will for the children of Israel (and us) to think of Him as the One who delivers us from slavery.

Why is it important for you to think of God in these terms?

How often do you need to remind yourself of this?

Parallel to these principles were two important points I heard at the recovery group: (1) Don't forget your last drink. (They weren't referring to the taste but rather my misery resulting from slavery to alcohol.) and (2) Your sobriety is contingent on your spiritual condition. (God was and is my deliverer.)

The children of Israel walked out of Egypt carrying their unleavened bread, belongings, and treasures given to them by the Egyptian people. They set up camp at the Red Sea where they were directed by God. Direction for the Israelites during their travels came via a pillar of cloud during the day and a pillar of fire at night (Exodus 13:21-22).

Meanwhile, back in Egypt, the Lord once again hardened Pharaoh's heart in regard to liberating the Hebrews. He "and his officials changed their minds about them and said, 'What have we done? We have let the Israelites go and have lost their services'" (Exodus 14:5).

In an attempt to bring them back, Pharaoh rode in his own

chariot with all his "horses and chariots, horsemen and troops" (Exodus 14:8).

Pharaoh was not coming after them with an engraved invitation to a picnic on the banks of the Nile River. Rather, being accompanied by his well-trained army made this the ultimate power play for Pharaoh. It was a matter of "my way or the highway" or more literally, life or death for the Israelites.

Earlier, we saw how things may become more difficult for us when we initially make a decision to worship God instead of idols. Now we see that after you turn your back on the land of slavery with every intention of leaving, Satan and/or his emissary may try to drag you back to the land of slavery. The enemy could come after you with power like "a roaring lion looking for someone to devour" (I Peter 5: 8), as "an angel of light" (II Corinthians 11:14), or quietly slither up beside you in the form of a snake as he did with Eve (Genesis 3:1).

In what ways have you been tempted to return to the slavery you thought you'd left behind you?

IT WAS PERSONAL

Though I was determined to leave the land of slavery, I was blind-sided one night by a long-time acquaintance, "Robert." This occurred when I had between three and four months of sobriety.

Robert's invitation sounded innocent enough. He called asking me to his house on a weeknight to play pinochle. Though not one of my best friends, I'd known Robert since high school and had attended quite a few parties at his house.

Arriving there, I learned that our card-playing partners were two young women with whom I was acquainted casually. One of them, Katie, I'd found attractive and upon seeing her there that night, hoped to make a good impression.

After a couple of games of cards, we sat around his kitchen table. They had beers in front of them but were not intoxicated. As per my recent custom, I was not drinking.

"Here, Don, have a brew." Robert held a cold can of beer in his hand. It made a snapping sound when he pulled off the tab top. He placed it down in front of me. "Drink it."

There I was in a social situation trying to make a good impression on Katie, circumstances very similar to why I'd first started drinking in high school. If I went ahead and started to imbibe, I would "go along to get along" and demonstrate to Katie I was still a regular guy.

Weighing in on the other side of the equation were things I'd learned from the recovery group. Namely, if I was an alcoholic, I could not handle even one beer. Over a period of time, the first drink would lead again to drunkenness and despair. It was possible, I knew, that going back to alcohol would kill me.

"No, thanks," I said to Robert.

"Come on, Don, why not have one?" he demanded more than asked.

Katie and her friend looked at me with anticipation. Robert was well aware of my recent stay in the mental hospital, and I'm sure these women were, too.

There was a moment of awkward silence.

Then I spoke up. "I'm not drinking it!" I stated it firmly and pushed the beer back toward him.

After that, Robert quit trying, and the social situation returned to a semblance of normality. I returned home that night still sober and with the knowledge of another person who did not have my best interests at heart, much like the bartender at the Golden Rooster who was mentioned in the first chapter.

I never again saw Katie, and it was more than two years later when I next encountered Robert. He was at a social gathering with a date.

"Meet Don," he said to her. "He's a guy who's found religion." I nodded affirmatively and smiled.

In what way has a "friend" attempted to drag you back toward slavery?

MUSTARD SEED-SIZED FAITH?

With Pharaoh's army bearing down on them, the children of Israel were pinned up against the Red Sea with nowhere to run. Terrified, they blurted out,

> *Weren't the cemeteries large enough in Egypt so that you had to take us out here in the wilderness to die? What have you done to us, taking us out of Egypt? Back in Egypt didn't we tell you this would happen? Didn't we tell you, "Leave us alone here in Egypt—we're better off as slaves in Egypt than as corpses in the wilderness"* (Exodus 14:11-12, *The Message*).

Before we read the response of Moses, let's pause for a quick observation. Some people say that they are disappointed in the panic among the Hebrews. They believe that if they had witnessed the 10 plagues, they would have had much greater faith in God under the same circumstances. Hmmmm.

If the same plagues occurred today for the same reason, our Godless culture would explain how these things had occurred naturally without any intervention from any outside force, just as all miracles in the Bible are dismissed by liberal scholars.

With a powerful army coming to drag you back into slavery or kill you, is it possible that you would have at least some doubt that God would save you?

Just asking.

Now let's see how Moses responded to the panic-stricken children of Israel.

> *Do not be afraid. Stand firm and you will see the deliverance the Lord will bring you today. The Egyptians you see today you will never see again. The Lord will fight for you; you need only to be still (Exodus 14:13-14).*

Don't miss what you just read. What did the children of Israel have to do to defeat a well-equipped army that by all appearances could crush them easily? Absolutely nothing! God would do the fighting for them.

When the going starts to get tough, it is so easy to want to do something—anything!!—in an attempt to gain a measure of control. With God in charge, sometimes the right action is inaction.

When has faith in God and inaction on your part been the best possible solution?

The Bible does not record the reaction of the Israelites to the assurances of Moses. Did they sleep well that night? Probably not. But even then, God kept the Egyptian army at a distance by placing the pillar of cloud between the two camps.

Following God's instructions,

> *Moses stretched out his hand over the sea, and all that night the Lord drove the sea back with a strong east wind and turned it into dry land. The waters were divided, and the Israelites went through the sea on dry ground with a wall of water on their right and on their left (Exodus 14:21-22).*

"The Egyptians pursued them, and all Pharaoh's horses and chariots and horsemen followed them into the sea" (Exodus 14:23). The Lord "made the wheels of their chariots come off, so that they had difficulty driving" (Exodus 14:25).

The soldiers then recognized that they were fighting against God. They tried to escape, but it was too late. "The water flowed back and covered the chariots and horsemen—the entire army of Pharaoh that had followed the Israelites into the sea. Not one of them survived" (Exodus 14:28).

The scene from the paragraph above was depicted in the 1956 movie *The Ten Commandments* starring Charleton Heston as Moses and Yul Brynner as Pharaoh. The film's last view of Brynner has him standing on the edge of the sea as it comes crashing down on his army. Based on this, you get the idea that Pharaoh survived, leaving him to return home as a broken man with no remaining vestiges of credibility.

Some scholars speculate that Pharaoh drowned with his soldiers.

The Bible, though, is silent on the fate of Pharaoh. In fact, the Bible does not even give Pharaoh's name. Perfectly clear, though, is that he was a man personally doomed by his unrelenting pride that resulted in destruction throughout his domain, including people, soldiers, animals and crops in addition to the debunking of his gods.

Rabbi Kahanov penned the following about this incident:

> *True, Pharaoh was driven by an exaggerated self-image and distorted sense of reality. He smugly defied G-d's demand, believing he would outsmart and outplay Him. Still, in face of the relentless and devastating afflictions he should have acquiesced. Even if he was only partially coherent he should have discerned that by now he was hopelessly out-gunned.*
>
> *While this would no doubt inflict a formidable blow to his royal ego, it would at least have spared him from the total annihilation suffered at the Red Sea where he forfeited every remaining vestige of honor and national glory. What could he have been thinking? The answer is that he wasn't.*[2]

I would add that Pharaoh had allowed himself to become a puppet of Satan. Like any person whose only purpose of repentance is to remove the heat he/she is feeling at the moment and then continues in denial on a path away from God, Pharaoh's self-destruction was complete.

Exodus 14 which relates the account of the Red Sea parting concludes like this:

> *That day the Lord saved Israel from the hands of the Egyptians, and Israel saw the Egyptians lying dead on the shore. And when the Israelites saw the great power the Lord displayed against the Egyptians, the people feared the Lord and put their trust in him and in Moses his servant (Exodus 14:30-31).*

How long would this act of God sustain the faith of the children of Israel? Keep reading.

Part II: Into the Desert

I will take you out of the nations;

I will gather you from all the countries and bring you back

into your own land. I will sprinkle clean water on you,

and you will be clean; I will cleanse you

from all your impurities and from all your idols.

I will give you a new heart and put a new spirit in you;

I will remove from you your

heart of stone and give you a heart of flesh.

Ezekiel 36:24-26

CHAPTER NINE

Big Changes

Having successfully crossed the Red Sea, the children of Israel found themselves in the desert of the Sinai Peninsula.

"The desert destroys affectation; it demands authenticity..." wrote Bruce Feiler in describing his attempt to trace the route followed by the children of Israel. "Come with a vague sense of identity; leave with a deeper sense of self."[1]

I agree with Feiler's observation but with a huge postscript. The desert itself does not give you a deeper sense of your identity. This comes only from God as you rely on Him during your desert journey.

Like the Israelites, we enter the desert with the idea that God will deliver us, but in many respects we continue to hold on to our old identities, the ones we had in the land of slavery. The children of Israel thought of themselves as pawns of Pharaoh. My arrogance told me I was a macho two-fisted drinker, gambler and ladies man, which today sounds like a poorly developed character in a low-budget movie.

What is/was your slave identity?
How do these old or current self-definitions
square up with the fact that we are made in God's image?

Here's what Feiler wrote about the journey ahead of the Hebrews:

> *Especially for a population that had grown up in the terminal lowland of the Nile Delta, the Sinai would have been a tease. First they would have come upon the dunes of the north, which themselves would have felt large for flatlanders. Then they would have arrived at the central hills, which at two thousand feet must have seemed daunting. And finally they would have faced the southern mountains, a formidable seven thousand feet high, which must have made even the "stiff-necked" Israelites crane with awe—and fear.*[2]

Clearly, this is a daunting journey for people accustomed to residing in the land of slavery. We enter the desert with little idea about what lies immediately in front of us and only vague notions of what it would be like to arrive in the Promised Land. We don't have GPS or even a road map. We must trust in God's guidance.

It is a certainty that people who depend on their slave-world definitions of self never will make it. They will either return to the land of slavery or die in the desert.

AVOID U-TURNS

When Pharaoh and his army were closing in on the children of Israel at the Red Sea, Moses said to them, "Do not be afraid. Stand firm and you will see the deliverance the Lord will bring you today. *The Egyptians you see today you will never see again*" (Exodus 14:13, emphasis mine).

A warning about not returning to the land of slavery is unequivocal in the book of Deuteronomy, a sermon or series of sermons by Moses delivered to the children of the children of Israel before they actually stepped into the Promised Land.

For example, in specifying qualifications for a king to rule over them at some point in the future, Moses stated, "The king moreover, must not acquire great numbers of horses for himself or make the people return to Egypt to get more of them, for the Lord has told you, 'You are not to go back that way again'" (Deuteronomy 17:16).

This prohibition was later to be ignored by King Solomon. (See I Kings 10:26-29; II Chronicles 1:16-17; 9:28.)

The warning about returning to slavery in Egypt is also mentioned among the possible consequences of disobedience to God spelled out by Moses. "The Lord will send you back in ships to Egypt on a journey I said you should never make again. There you will offer yourselves for sale to your enemies as male and female slaves, but no one will buy you" (Deuteronomy 28:68). (Also see Isaiah 31:1; Jeremiah 42:13-19; Ezekiel 17:15-18; 23:27.)

The horrible ramifications of reverting to past spiritual slavery are also found in the New Testament as demonstrated in this passage:

> *If they have escaped the corruption of the world by knowing our Lord and Savior Jesus Christ and are again entangled in it and overcome, they are worse off at the end than they were at the beginning. It would have been better for them not to have known the way of righteousness, than to have known it and then to turn their backs*

on the sacred command that was passed on to them. Of them the proverbs are true: "A dog returns to its vomit" (Proverbs 26:11), and "A sow that is washed goes back to her wallowing in the mud" (II Peter 2:20-22).

Progressive effects of alcoholism are discussed at recovery meetings. This means that for an alcoholic, the negative results of drinking compound with the passage of time. Now get this: The compounding effect occurs *whether or not* the alcoholic stays sober or continues drinking. In other words, if an alcoholic sobered up and stayed that way for five years, the detrimental ramifications of drinking would be the same as if that person had been drinking the whole time.

I've seen this in the lives of many people with whom I've been acquainted, including a university dean and a chiropractor who each drank himself to death.

This phenomenon also has basis in the following words of Jesus Christ:

*When a defiling evil spirit is expelled from someone, it drifts along through the desert looking for an oasis, some unsuspecting soul it can bedevil. When it doesn't find anyone, it says, "I'll go back to my old haunt." On return it finds the person spotlessly clean, but vacant. It then runs out and rounds up seven other spirits more evil than itself and they all move in, whooping it up. That person ends up far worse off than if he'd never gotten cleaned up in the first place (*Matthew 12:43-45, *The Message).*

The vacancy mentioned in this passage means that God is not present.

I've heard it said that nature fills voids, and that is the case here. This principle applies to any number of sins/addictions.

MOVING VAN UNNECESSARY

Unlike the children of Israel, we may or may not experience a geographic change when we decide to leave the land of slavery and enter the desert. Rather, our metaphorical desert journey occurs as we attempt to leave our old idols behind and rely completely on God. Our goal is to put spiritual, mental, and (in many cases) physical distance between our idols and ourselves.

This is a life-long journey.

In his book *The Land Between,* Jeff Manion used the desert journey of the Israelites to describe difficult times faced by Christians and how God can use our troubles in a positive way. Here are some of his conclusions:

- *"The Land Between can be profoundly disorienting. It also provides the space for God to do some of his deepest work in our lives."*

- *"God intends for us to emerge from this land radically reshaped."*

- *"The conditions can prove so harsh that there seems little room for neutrality." The journey "usually forces us to choose one way or the other."*

- *"While offering us a greenhouse for growth, the Land Between can also be a desert where our faith goes to die." Our choices during this journey "will determine whether the Land Between results in spiritual life or spiritual death."*[3]

The initial part of my trip included plenty of peaks and a whole lot of valleys; sometimes, the distance between them was mighty short. One moment I was flying high and congratulating myself on my newfound sobriety but shortly thereafter I felt like I was trudging through the valley of death.

I welcomed those high peaks at first but came to recognize them as manic stages that were just as bad as the low points. A worthwhile goal, I learned, was to live so that my highs were not so high and that my lows were not so low.

"Do you want to get well?" (John 5:6) This was a question asked by Jesus to a man at the pool of Bethesda who'd been an invalid for 38 years. An answer of yes would require a complete change in this man's identity and lifestyle. The alternative for him was to remain without the ability to walk and stay by thc pool with other handicapped people, a life to which he was accustomed. Apparently, the man did want change because Jesus healed him and the man moved on.

If the Lord had asked if I wanted to get well, I usually would have answered affirmatively, but I was sometimes overwhelmed by discouragement.

Have you ever grappled with the notion that it would be easier to stay exactly where you are and not even attempt to make spiritual improvements?

Author Jack Zavata wrote on the topic of making change in one's life. I identify with what he wrote. See if you do.

> *Change is hard—so hard, in fact, that most of us avoid it at all costs.*
>
> *But by avoiding change, we create even bigger problems, such as lost opportunities, broken relationships, or sometimes a wasted life. Millions of people who need to change are drifting along with no real purpose, no joy, feeling as if they're traveling a dead end street.*

I can relate. I've had to make some major changes in my life, and each time they were painful. I usually fought those changes until I reached my misery threshold, then I reluctantly did something rash to escape the bad situation.

Each time I needed to make a change, I was afraid because I didn't know what was coming. Like most people, I like predictability. I thrive on sureness. Change means stepping into the unknown and losing your comfortable routine, and that's frightening.

I also knew that to a large degree, I had to give up control. That's scary too. Sure, I prepared as well as I could, but I couldn't run everything. Change involves so many factors that you just can't manipulate all of them.

When you're not in control, you lose your sense of invulnerability. You quickly realize you're not as powerful as you thought. That bravery you put so much pride in seems to evaporate when you realize you're not the one in charge any more.[4]

Control is also a factor in literature from the program of Alcoholics Anonymous. Readers are asked to draw the three conclusions below applied to alcoholics (with my added comments following in parentheses) that relate to anyone's desert journey with slight changes of wording.

(It is important to understand:)

a. "That we were alcoholic and could not manage our own lives." (This identifies the problem or the idol, and shows that in order to move forward, the person confessing this has little or no control.);

b. "That probably no human power could have relieved our alcoholism." (This includes doctors, psychologists and psychiatrists, moms, dads, ministers or any other person on the face of the earth, including you.);

c. "That God could and would if He were sought."[5] ("Ask and it will be given to you; seek and you will find; knock and the door will be opened to you. For everyone who asks receives; he who seeks finds; and to him who knocks, the door will be opened") (Matthew 7:7-8).

A PRAYER FOR HELP

One night during the early months of my sobriety just before going to bed, I got on my knees and prayed that God would take away my anxieties. Not noticing any improvement during the days that followed, I felt like my prayer had fallen on deaf ears. It took me a long time to discover that I was wrong about that.

Avner Goren, who served as author Feiler's guide in tracing the footsteps of the Israelites, reasoned that God's purpose of the Exodus was to strengthen the people so that they would be able to conquer the inhabitants of the Promised Land when they arrived there.[6] This corresponds with ideas relating to spiritual fitness.

God's answer to my prayer was not *yes* and not *no*---it was *not yet*. In effect, I had asked God to give me wings so I could fly over the desert without difficulty. If God had done this—and He certainly could have—I would have learned nothing about the spiritual bankruptcy that landed me in the mental hospital. For me, the ongoing challenges of the desert turned out to be a part of my metamorphosis from a life characterized by self-will run riot toward a focus on God's will and service to others.

The desert thus serves a positive purpose. Here is what Moses told the children of Israel as they were finally about to enter the Promised Land:

> *Remember how the Lord your God led you all the way in the desert these forty years, to humble you and to test you in order to know what was in your heart, whether or not you would keep his commands (Deuteronomy 8:2).*

In the next chapter we'll look at the first bump in the road encountered by the children of Israel as they entered the desert.

CHAPTER TEN

Here's to Your Health

In the midst of two places to find drinking water in the desert, the children of Israel received a message from God that has huge ramifications in our lives today. Like water in the desert, this promise from God is life-giving.

Having just crossed the Red Sea safely, the children of Israel praised God for delivering them from Pharaoh's army. A testament to their new-found faith is recorded in Exodus 15, "The Song of Moses and Miriam."

Then after traveling three days into the desert without finding water, they started singing a different song.

Their hopes must have been riding high when they saw water in the distance at a place known as Marah. That name means bitter,[1] which describes the condition of the water there. When they tasted it, "the people grumbled against Moses, saying, 'What are we to drink?'" (Exodus 15:24)

This is the first—but certainly not the last—recorded instance of grumbling during this journey and the different song to which I alluded.

Moses knew he didn't have the power to make the water drinkable, so he prayed. "The Lord showed him a piece of wood. He threw it into the water, and the water became sweet" (Exodus 15:25).

After that, "They came to Elim, where there were twelve springs and seventy palm trees, and they camped there near the water" (Exodus 15:27).

GOD'S PLAN

In between those stops, "the Lord made a decree and a law for them, and he tested them" (Exodus 15:25). Here is what the Lord said,

> *If you listen carefully to the voice of the Lord your God and do what is right in his eyes, if you pay attention to his commands and keep all his decrees, I will not bring on you any of the diseases I brought on the Egyptians, for I am the Lord, who heals you (Exodus 15:26).*

As you can see, God's word specifies a relationship between one's relationship with Him and good health. This relationship continues today.

It was news to me when I learned about this at the recovery group. They said that my spiritual condition had a direct bearing on both my physical and mental health.

Based on what I had observed in my own life in the preceding years, this concept made sense. Here's why: I was guilty repeatedly of the sin of drunkenness (a spiritual disease). This had created both mental and physical problems for me. You already know about the mental part, but my physical problems first came to light when I was 21. That's when our family doctor told me I had high blood pressure resulting from drinking. Five years later, I was diagnosed with an enlarged liver, a step on the way to cirrhosis.

The fact that I continued drinking in spite of these warnings is a testament to the depth of my denial, which would itself seem to be a mental disease with a spiritual basis.

The link between spiritual and mental/physical has been lost on our culture due to the wide-spread adherence of modernism, which denies that we are spiritual beings made in the image of God. Medical training includes treatment for physical problems, and both psychiatrists and psychologists address mental problems, but most overlook spiritual solutions.

As an example, suppose a seventh grader dies tragically after being hit by a car on the way to school. A generation or two earlier, clergy members would have been called to console grieving students. When such a tragedy occurs today, however, the media dutifully report that grief counselors were called to help. These people are trained in psychological methods.

Many Christians have absorbed this world view that excludes God and may not even recognize it as a form of idolatry in their lives. Clearly, though, ties between the spiritual, mental, and physical are found throughout the Bible.

For example, the Fifth Commandment, "Honor your father and your mother…" contains a promise related to longevity, "… so that you may live long in the land the Lord your God is giving you" (Exodus 20:12; Deuteronomy 5:16).

Speaking to God in a Psalm, David wrote,

> *Your hand has come down upon me. Because of your wrath there is no health in my body; my bones have no soundness because of my sin. My guilt has overwhelmed me like a burden too heavy to bear... All day long I go about mourning. My back is filled with searing pain; there is no health in my body. I am feeble and utterly crushed; I groan in anguish of heart (Psalm 38:2-4,6-8).*

To a man who had been healed, Jesus said, "See, you are well again. Stop sinning or something worse may happen to you" (John 5:14).

The failure of Christians to judge their own actions when eating the bread and drinking the cup of communion prompted Paul to write, "That's why so many of you even now are listless and sick, and others have gone to an early grave" (I Corinthians 11:30, *The Message*).

Finally, here's a verse about the mental effects of over-indulgence in alcohol that describes what happened to me: "Your eyes will see strange sights and your mind imagine confusing things" (Proverbs 23:33).

For other examples, see Exodus 22:25-26; Deuteronomy 5:32-33; 28:22,28,60,66-67; Psalm 34:12-14; Proverbs 3:7-8; Proverbs 4:10, 20-22; 10:27; II Samuel 13:1-2; Ezekiel 20:43; and Ephesians 4:22-23.

Clearly, there's a connection between spiritual health and both mental and physical health, but it is important to observe that such a link does not always exist. For example, Jesus was asked whether the cause of a man being born blind resulted from the sin of that man or his parents. "Neither," the Lord replied, "This happened that the work of God might be displayed in his life" (John 9:3).

Also unrelated to spiritual fitness today are organic causes for mental and physical maladies.

Bad things also happen to good people. See Luke 13:1-5 and the story of Uriah the Hittite in II Samuel 11.

MOSES'S PRESCRIPTION

"Moses was educated in all the wisdom of the Egyptians and was powerful in speech and action" (Acts 7:22). Spending his first 40 years in an Egyptian royal household, he would have been very familiar with the medical practices of Egypt, known to be the best in the world.

In dispensing medical advice for the Israelites that would be preserved in scriptures, would Moses rely on what he'd learned in Egypt or divine guidance? He took the spiritual path.

Egyptian medical practices are preserved in what is known as the Ebers Papyrus that dates back to around 1500 B.C., the approximate time of Moses. Information contained in this document is believed to have been an accumulation of medical wisdom over a period of many centuries. The papyrus was in the form of a scroll said to have been found entombed with a mummy. It became known to the western world when purchased for a collection in 1862.[2]

The Ebers Papyrus includes some medical advice that still may be considered valid today. For example, the treatment for asthma included "a mixture of herbs heated on a brick so that the sufferer could inhale their fumes."[3]

On the other hand, a cure for pinkeye was to "apply the urine of a faithful wife."[4]

Prescriptions included the following: "statue dust, beetle shells, mouse tails, cat hair, pig eyes, dog toes, breast milk, human semen, eel eyes and goose guts."[5]

What is your treatment for a splinter? Ancient Egyptian doctors would have applied a salve. You might automatically think of an antibiotic ointment because of the dangers of infection. But for millennia up until the late 1800s, doctors thought that healing would come after pus was produced. Toward this end, the salve used by Egyptians was a mixture of worm blood and donkey dung; this latter ingredient contains tetanus spores, ultimately causing the death of many trusting patients.[6]

As I write this in December 2010, a cholera epidemic has spread to more than 100,000 Haitians during the preceding two months. This followed a devastating earthquake that left people living in crowded, make-shift housing without provisions for the disposal of human waste. The disease is spread through the ingestion of water (and food in contact with this water) that is contaminated with untreated sewage or human feces.

Here's God's prescription in the Law of Moses to prevent the spread of cholera: "Designate a place outside the camp where you can go to relieve yourself. As part of your equipment have something to dig with, and when you relieve yourself, dig a hole and cover up your excrement" (Deuteronomy 23:12-13).

Drs. S. I. McMillen and David E. Stern describe that the methods of hand-washing for sterilization recommended by the U.S. Centers for Disease Control are parallel to those written by Moses in Numbers 19.[7]

Quite clearly, God's prescription for healthy living revealed by

Moses was revolutionary in the ancient world.

For more examples of God's health revelations in the Law of Moses, I highly recommend the book by S. I. McMillen and David E. Stern, titled *None of These Diseases: The Bible's Health Secrets for the 21st Century*, Fleming H. Revell, Grand Rapids, MI, 2000.

ABSORBING MY CULTURE

As I stayed sober and entered my desert journey, I had no idea about the extent to which I was being bogged down by slave-world ideas that deny we are spiritual in nature.

I was spoon-fed Darwin's theory of evolution by my ninth grade biology teacher, one of the most likeable and popular teachers at our school. One day, he said, "Raise your hand if you believe in a literal Adam and Eve as the first human beings." Based on the way it was stated, it seemed that anyone who raised a hand would be classified as an idiot. Though I did believe in a literal Adam and Eve, I had no intention of being the only idiot present. Since not a single hand was raised, apparently no one else did, either.

We were taught that the classification of animals into phyla was a verification of one species of animal evolving into another, an idea that seemed like proof-positive to a 14-year-old but does not hold a drop of water from a scientific standpoint.

We also learned about the notion of ontogeny recapitulates phylogeny, which means that prior to their birth, people and animals go through all of the earlier stages of evolution. My sister was taught the same thing several years later at Michigan State University. Come to find out, this idea was based on some faked drawings by Darwin apologist Ernst Haeckel and had been disproved decades earlier.[8]

As I was growing up, the Salk vaccine put an end to the crippling disease of polio. President Kennedy said we would put a man on the moon within the decade, and we did. Undoubtedly, there were hundreds of messages that led me to believe there were no limits to what humanity could accomplish.

If man could achieve so much, where did God fit in? This is not the type of question I would have asked as a teenager, but pieces of this puzzle must have been rumbling around in the corners of my psyche.

The answer for me ended up being that God did not fit in anywhere. Guiding my decision-making about God was a heavy dose of pornography starting in my early teens and the idol of alcohol.

I made a conscious decision to rid myself of any vestiges of my old-time religion. I could not continue believing in God while maintaining behaviors I knew were wrong. Something had to go, and I chose to keep idolatry. That's when I started suffering from anxiety and other problems.

At that time, it never would have occurred to me to turn to a minister for help.

You may not have used pornography or alcohol the way I did, but you have lived in a culture that excludes your spiritual nature.

To what extent have you been impacted by modernist thought that denies our spiritual selves? Have you carried this idol into your desert journey?

Below are three examples demonstrating the results in our society of excluding God's wisdom.

THE COST OF STRESS

If you are seeking peace in your life, look to the Lord. Jesus told His disciples, "Peace I leave with you; my peace I give you. I do not give to you as the world gives. Do not let your hearts be troubled and do not be afraid" (John 14:27).

On the same subject Paul, wrote,

> *Do not be anxious about anything, but in everything, by prayer and petition, with thanksgiving, present your requests to God. And the peace of God which transcends all understanding, will guard your hearts and your minds in Christ Jesus (Philippians 4:6-7).*

Do you believe that the stressed-out society in which we reside has "the peace of God?"

According to a national health survey, 75% of the general population experiences at least "some stress" every two weeks with half of those respondents reporting moderate or high levels. Stress is so common that the U.S. Public Health Service has made stress-reduction a major health-promotion goal.[9]

Stress is associated with the following health problems: heart disease, heart attack, high blood pressure, stroke, diabetes, cancer, ulcers, irritable bowel syndrome, rheumatoid arthritis, insomnia, chronic fatigue, depression, obesity, cancer, muscle aches, and memory loss.[10]

Stress also affects the immune system and contributes to the development of numerous addictions.[11]

How does the stress level in your life compare to "the peace of God which transcends all understanding?" (Philippians 4:6) What do you plan to do about this?

HOW SAFE IS IT?

"Safe sex" by the world's standards is the use of a condom, but the Word of God tells us that the only safe (and condoned) sex is a monogamous marital relationship between a man and a woman, which the Bible describes as being "one flesh" (Ephesians 5:31).

According to Kenneth L. Boles, this "goes far beyond the physical union, encompassing the blending together of every facet of the two lives. The sharing of bodies is accompanied by the sharing of minds, spirits, hopes, needs, aspirations."[12]

Paul wrote about the spiritual component of the sexual union in marriage as "a profound mystery...Christ and the church" (Ephesians 5: 23).

Looking at it from a modern or post-modern perspective, sex is simply the sharing of body parts; when and with whom this might occur is dependent on finding a willing adult partner who has a body part desirable to the person doing the seeking.

This has led us to a point where each year there are an estimated 19 million new cases of sexually transmitted diseases (STDs) in the U.S., according to the U.S. Centers for Disease Control.[13] Those most apt to be infected are ages 15 to 24.[14]

For years, condoms have been distributed to teens as a part of sex education, but if condoms and education are the solution, why have STDs skyrocketed during the same time frame?

In 1960, there were the five STDs. The most well known were gonorrhea and syphilis. Today there are over 20 STDs.[15]

Though the deadly HIV-AIDS virus seems to get the most publicity, the human papilloma virus (HPV) is the most commonly transmitted STD. It includes between 80 and 100 strains of the virus, some producing cancer of the cervix, anus, mouth and throat.[16] Other STDs result in infertility, various forms of hepatitis, and liver cancer.

Homosexuals are in the highest risk group for the most serious STDs.[17]

In what ways have your attitudes and behaviors been affected by our culture's perspectives on sex?
In answering this question, be sure to include the content of the movies you attend, television programs you watch, what you see on the internet, and jokes which you tell or hear.

GROWING IN GIRTH

Just about every time I turn on the television or look at billboards along the Interstate Highway closest to my home, I see advertising for lap-band surgery aimed at weight reduction. This type of surgery has not always been so highly hyped. Why now?

The U.S. obesity rate nearly doubled between 1995 and 2010, going from 15.9% in 1995 to 27.6% in 2010. It is different by state, ranging from lowest (21%) in Colorado to the highest (34%) in Mississippi.[18]

> *Obesity is most commonly caused by a combination of excessive food energy intake, lack of physical activity, and genetic susceptibility, although a few cases are caused primarily by genes, endocrine disorders, medications or psychiatric illness.*[19]

Obesity is measured in terms of the ratio between height and girth, but the bottom line is that it is associated with numerous health problems often leading to a shorter life span. These include heart disease, high blood pressure, stroke, diabetes, and leg and back problems. Concurrent with obesity are feelings of worthlessness and depression.[20]

The projected future medical costs for treating effects of obesity are astronomical.[21]

What is the solution?

In our secular world, I hear a lot of calls for nutritious eating, and they are worth heeding. But I rarely hear anyone say that continual overeating is a spiritual disease and a form of idolatry.

Paul wrote of those who "make their bellies their gods; belches are their praise; all they can think of is their appetites" (Philippians 3:18-19, *The Message).*

A warning about gluttony also is found in Proverbs. "Put a knife to your throat if you are given to gluttony." (Proverbs 23:2) and "Do not join those who drink too much wine or gorge themselves on meat, for drunkards and gluttons become poor, and drowsiness clothes them in rags" (Proverbs 23:20-21).

Food becomes an idol when people try to place it into the God-shaped hole in their heart that only God can fill, such as I did with alcohol, a Corvette—the list goes on.

To what extent is food an idol in your life?

CHAPTER ELEVEN

Manna Lessons

Six weeks after crossing the Red Sea on dry ground and watching the water close in over the Egyptian army, the children of Israel started thinking about "the good ol' days" back in Egypt. They'd earlier grumbled about water, but now their focus was on food.

Finding themselves in the Desert of Sin, the Israelites complained to Moses and Aaron. "If only we had died by the Lord's hand in Egypt! There we sat around pots of meat and ate all the food we wanted, but you have brought us out into this desert to starve this entire assembly to death" (Exodus 16:3).

Apparently, they used selective memories to block out the horrors of slavery and the fact that God had both delivered them and provided for their needs.

Satan, the father of lies, is the only possible source for self-deception that includes remembering slavery in a positive manner. The children of Israel aren't the only ones to fall prey to this form of denial. Just about all people attempting to leave their idols behind them will have positive memories—either real or imagined—of slave life.

During my senior year of high school and first year of college, my drinking experiences seemed mostly positive. They included a lot of laughs with friends. As things started to go bad for me, I tried vainly to recapture those experiences. Maybe this is one reason the recovery group stressed remembering my last drink—not my first.

What positive memories do you have from idolatry? Why are they a lie?

With the Israelites grumbling about food, God did not dress them down for their ingratitude. Rather, God's message to His children through Moses was that He would provide their food. "Then you will know that I am the Lord your God" (Exodus 16:12).

That night, He presented them with a feast of quail. The next morning, the Israelites woke up and saw a layer of dew around them. "When the dew was gone, thin flakes like frost on the ground appeared on the desert floor" (Exodus 16:14). The Israelites did not know that this was manna, food from God.

Scholars are not sure about the derivation of the Hebrew word that we translate as "manna." It may mean "What is it?" or "Is it food?"[1]

Moses told them, "It is the bread the Lord has given you to eat" (Exodus 16:15).

Attempts to find a natural explanation for the appearance of this substance has eluded experts,[2] but of course, there have been attempts. Author Bruce Feiler, for example, observed that manna most likely resulted from the spring-time secretions of tamarisk trees that grow around many oases.[3]

This perspective does not account for the fact that manna appeared on the ground *year-round* for the next 40 years and that it did not appear on Saturdays. Furthermore, after all that time in Egypt, the children of Israel wouldn't have had to ask about the identity of manna if it came from tamarisk trees. Scripture is clear that manna was something their "fathers had never known" (Deuteronomy 8:16).

There are always those who attribute the work of God's hands to coincidence or some other natural process. Following their logic, you might soon reach a conclusion that everything in this universe came together without God (which, of course, is a belief of modernism).

What manna lessons can we take with us?

1. GOD MEETS THE NEEDS OF HIS PEOPLE.

The task of the Israelites was to pick up the manna that God provided. This required some effort because they couldn't simply lie on their backs and let the manna fly into their mouths.

They didn't have to plant, cultivate, dig, or climb for it. And the end result seemed to have nothing to do with effort exerted. "Some gathered much, some little... He who gathered much did not have too much, and he who gathered little did not have too little" (Exodus 16:17-18).

As Moses was to tell the Israelites before they entered the Promised Land, "He gave you manna to eat in the desert... to humble and to test you so that in the end it might go well with you" (Deuteronomy 8:16).

The humbling comes from a knowledge of God-dependence instead of self-reliance.

Our equivalent of manna is that we look to God to supply the things that life requires. "Seek first his kingdom and his righteousness, and all these things will be given to you as well" (Matthew 6:33).

It is easy to fall into the trap of slave-world thinking that our blessings result from our own efforts.

Again, quoting Moses's sermon toward the end of the wilderness journey, "You may say to yourself, 'My power and the strength of my hands have produced this wealth for me.' But remember the Lord your God, for it is he who gives you the ability to produce wealth..." (Deuteronomy 8:17-18).

Thankfully, God meets our needs but does not promise to provide for our wants. He knows us better than we know ourselves. Our acknowledgment of this allows Him to work in our lives.

What are some of your needs? Your wants? Looking at your past, how are you now better off for not having received some specific wants?

2. MANNA IS USUALLY PROVIDED DAILY.

Related to the manna experience was Jesus's petition in the Lord's prayer, "Give us today our daily bread" (Matthew 6:11).

Like manna, God provides on a *daily* basis. This includes

both our needs and the strength to avoid harmful things.

Today—in fact, this very moment—is the only period of time over which we have any control. We have no control over what happened yesterday or will occur tomorrow. In the words of Jesus, "Do not worry about tomorrow, for tomorrow will worry about itself. Each day has enough trouble of its own" (Matthew 6:34).

Moses reinforced this idea after the children of Israel had gathered manna the first time. He told them not to keep any of it until the next morning. "However, some of them paid no attention to Moses; they kept part of it until morning, but it was full of maggots and began to smell" (Exodus 16:20).

Day-old manna may represent our pasts. These are the thoughts and memories we carry with us from all of our yesterdays. Discernment is needed to determine what to take with us and what to discard. If we lug the wrong things into tomorrow, we will become spiritually stinky.

The Bible speaks plainly about something that should not be carried over into the next day: "... Do not let the sun go down while you are still angry..." (Ephesians 4:26). Why not? It will "give the devil a foothold" (Ephesians 4:27).

Today's anger becomes tomorrow's resentment, which means literally to "re-feel." Resentments have a way of becoming false gods. When our feelings are hurt, we are offended, or our egos bruised whether yesterday or 50 years ago—we "re-feel" this pain when we think about the incident. Suddenly, our minds and bodies react as though it just happened, and there we are burning with anger once again—reacting to the past, plotting vengeance, and self-destructing.

To prevent this, Jesus instructed His followers to deal with anger and personal conflicts today.

If you are offering your gift at the altar and there remember that your brother has something against you, leave your gift there in front of the altar. First go and be reconciled to your brother; then come and offer your gift (Matthew 5:23-24).

Besides past conflicts and pains, our victories may or may not be a good thing to carry with us. Will they be used as excuses to rest on our laurels or as stepping stones for future success?

How have you used past victories toward great successes in the future? How have you used them as an excuse to stop moving forward?

Certainly, we do not want to forget where we came from (slavery) and who is delivering us (God). In fact, God can use the worst parts of our slave lives for good, and this has been true for me. Much of my personal ministry is based on helping those with addictions. (How many authors tell you about drinking themselves into a mental hospital?)

How can God use your greatest weaknesses and past defeats to help others? What would prevent you from letting Him?

3. ULTIMATELY, THE SHELF LIFE OF MANNA IS DETERMINED BY GOD.

On Fridays, God told His people to gather enough for both that day and the next because manna would not appear on Saturdays. This was an apparent precursor of the Sabbath rest. "Nevertheless, some of the people went out on the seventh day to gather it, but they found none" (Exodus 16:27).

Those who didn't follow God's instructions were hungry all day Saturday. We can become spiritually hungry when we ignore Godly direction.

What is worthwhile for us to carry with us from today into tomorrow? "Whatever is true, whatever is noble, whatever is right, whatever is pure, whatever is lovely, whatever is admirable..." (Philippians 4:8).

The idea that manna might be accessible now but not later might be translated in our lives as windows of opportunity that exist at specific periods of our lives.

What are some opportunities that people have only at certain stages of life?

GOD EVICTS ANOTHER IDOL

The network television news had my full attention as it relayed the following message from health experts: People between the ages of 30 and 35 who smoke two packs of cigarettes daily can expect, on average, to die between eight and 10 years sooner than if they didn't smoke at all.

Nearing age 33, I was over five years sober but had been a heavy smoker since inhaling my first cigarette 14 years earlier. The thought was frightening that I would reach a point where my health would be damaged irreparably due to my inability to stop smoking. I wondered how many victims of lung cancer or emphysema had wished they'd stopped earlier.

After watching the news report that night, January 11, 1979,

I took a quick look at my cigarette inventory. I had one left in a pack. I smoked it and have not had another cigarette since.

Due to my self-discipline, I immediately was able to take action on the television news story to stop smoking. Right?

Wrong. Self-discipline had failed in several earlier, very earnest attempts to stop smoking.

To help me get over the uncomfortable craving after that last cigarette, I went out and bought some smokeless tobacco. I planned to use this product for a week or two. (Yes, I was in denial, as you will soon see.)

Even with the use of snuff, I continued to long for a cigarette. To guide me away from that first smoke, I tried to employ the principle of living one day at a time. I'd first learned about this from the recovery group. I was told that it wasn't necessary—or even advisable—for me to make a vow to never drink again. Rather, was it possible for me to go one day without drinking? Sure, I could do that.

The idea was to ask God each morning to give me the strength to not drink that day and then repeat the same thing the next morning.

The cigarette habit was different, though, because it would be torture to go an entire day without lighting up. But it was possible to use the same principle by breaking the day into smaller increments. When I was tempted to smoke—which was continually, I would seek God while making a point to not reach out toward the idol. "During this very moment I will not smoke a cigarette," I would tell myself.

The moments piled up, and soon I had gone an hour, two

hours, and an entire day without smoking. Then the days multiplied. The longer I went without a cigarette, the less I thought of one. After a few months, the thought of smoking crossed my mind only occasionally.

The problem is that I continued using smokeless tobacco beyond the one or two weeks originally envisioned. I still was addicted to nicotine but rationalized that at least I wasn't smoking. While there had been plenty of news about the health dangers of cigarettes, at that time there was not much information about the down sides of snuff and chewing tobacco. To be perfectly honest, though, I was pretty sure such scientific data would be forthcoming, and that turned out to be true.

My use of snuff went from weeks to months to years. During two failed attempts to quit snuff, the cravings for nicotine were so great that I was unable to sleep at night.

I came to see that the idol nicotine cut me off from other people and also affected my Christian service. I was asked to join others on a mission trip to Russia but didn't go because of concerns about my ability to sneak off from missionary work to put a "peench" between my cheek and gum. What if I was stuck indoors with nowhere to spew my tobacco juice?

The financial aspects also galled me. The cost per can kept rising for something I would spit out, something that provided no benefit other than feed an addiction.

I set a date to quit nicotine that was a few months hence—the day after I turned in my students' grades for the spring 1995 semester. I prayed regularly for success. I reasoned that if God had created the universe, He could certainly give me the strength to endure the inevitable cravings. Nevertheless, I did not look forward to the discomfort of withdrawal.

This was the only time in my teaching career when I did not look forward to the end of the semester.

When the dreaded day arrived, I felt a void inside of me with a desire to fill it that was non-stop. For the first time in years, I felt like having a cigarette. I knew that either a cigarette or dip of snuff would give me a feeling of warmth throughout my entire being. I actually felt a sense of mourning for the loss of a "friend" that beckoned me to come back just one more time.

There were at least two lies associated with my temptation to return to nicotine, which means they were products of Satan.

The first was that nicotine was a friend. Actually, it was a wolf in sheep's clothing. This substance *seemed* to offer positive short-term effects but was actually harmful, even deadly, in the long term.

The second lie was that while trying to get off this substance, I could use nicotine just one more time. I earlier had succumbed to this falsehood many times when trying to quit either cigarettes or snuff, and I could see that "one more time" kept leading me toward an addiction that had continued for years beyond what my "ideal" self desired. By this time, I was 49 years old and could see that it easily could go on for a lifetime.

In order to cope, I prayed often and went back to not using for the present moment. Those moments have continued to pile up since May 1995. Each morning when I get on my knees for prayer, I thank God for giving me the strength to go through another day without alcohol or nicotine.

One unanticipated health benefit of quitting nicotine was that digestive problems I'd suffered for years all but disappeared.

The one-day-at-a-time principle is used by the numerous programs that deal with addictions. But you don't have to be a member of any such group to put this to work in your life.

What idol stands in the way of your being more Christ-like? Worry? Gossip? A bad temper? What else?

Pray each morning for God to give you the strength to not engage in this behavior or thought process for the moment, hour, and/or day. If you fail, repent and start again.

The ramifications of living one day at a time also may be applied to things we wish to accomplish.

What worthwhile activity has so far eluded you? Serving God at a level you didn't think possible? Finishing some schooling or embarking on a new level of education? Reading the Bible from cover to cover? Maintaining a better attitude at work? Living healthier? A better prayer life? What else?

No matter what, your approach always boils down to what you can do today.

CHAPTER TWELVE

There's a Word for It

When I was growing up in metropolitan Detroit, Michigan, our family made the same two trips quite a few times. One of them was about three hours north to my dad's birthplace, Bentley, Michigan. The other was a day and a half south to Bear Creek, Alabama, where my mother grew up.

Each destination had a great deal of appeal, including swimming and fishing with cousins plus plenty of aunts and uncles to dote over me.

The problem was getting there. When I was very young, I could not distinguish one trip from the other. Both seemed endless.

Like many children, I had little appreciation for the journey but rather was focused on the destination. Also like others, my most frequent question was, "When will we get there?"

Even though the children of Israel weren't just children, a particular incident during their trip to the Promised Land demonstrated child-like impatience, leading them to regress to godless behaviors from the land of slavery. This occurred after they set up camp in front of Mount Sinai three months after departing from Egypt.

Moses went up the mountain and met with the Lord in a dense cloud. From their vantage-point at the bottom, the people heard thunder and saw lightning and smoke come from the mountain and heard the increasingly louder sound of a trumpet. They "trembled with fear" (Exodus 20:18).

When Moses descended, the Israelites said to him, "Speak to us yourself and we will listen. But do not have God speak to us or we will die" (Exodus 20:19). After Moses gave them a report of God's words and law, the people responded, "Everything the Lord has said we will do" (Exodus 24:3).

Going up the mountain again, Moses disappeared into a cloud to receive the law and commandments on "tablets of stone inscribed by the finger of God" (Exodus 31:18). He stayed there for 40 days and 40 nights.

Waiting for him below, the Israelites apparently started thinking they'd stayed too long at this particular rest stop. They were anxious to get on down the road toward the Promised Land. They "gathered around Aaron and said, 'Come, make us gods who will go before us. As for this fellow Moses who brought us up out of Egypt, we don't know what has happened to him'" (Exodus 32:1).

Despite God's miracles and guidance and the leadership of Moses, the impatience of the Israelites led them to a willingness to jettison both the Lord and Moses in order to follow gods.

It's too bad the Israelites were not able to follow in the spirit of the old Texas expression, "You got to dance with them that brung you." Using this saying in a political discussion on television, Bob Gammage, former Texas Supreme Court justice, added the following warning that also applies here, "If you don't dance with them what brung you, you may not be there for the next dance."[1]

Based on the behaviors that followed, this was, indeed, the "last dance" for some of the Israelites.

In what ways have you sought out idols from your past because God's timeline on your life's journey did not match up with your own?

HIGH PRIEST, LOW DECISION

Moses's brother, Aaron, had been set aside as the high priest of Israel, making him and his descendants the nation's religious leader. This makes his response to the people's request to make gods all the more disappointing. He told them to take off their gold earrings, which he melted and fashioned into the shape of a calf. Some experts believe the golden calf was a likeness of the Apis bull, thought by Egyptians to have special powers as the incarnation of their god, Osiris.[2]

The actual Apis bull had very specific markings and was believed to have been conceived by a cow via a flash of lightning from heaven. When one was born, it was a time of great celebration, perhaps what the children of Israel soon would emulate.

The Apis calf was purified in a temple and given special treatment, including its own harem of heifers. The cow giving birth to this calf was associated with Isis and also considered sacred. When Apis bulls died, they were mummified. Egyptians then eagerly awaited the arrival of the next Apis.[3]

Seeing the golden calf that Aaron had made, the Israelites said, "These are your gods, O Israel, who brought you up out of Egypt" (Exodus 32:4).

This all seems like a very straightforward case for idolatry on the part of both Aaron and the people, a violation of the First Commandment ("You shall have no other gods before me." Exodus 20:3). However, the two passages that follow throw a monkey wrench into the idea that the people wanted to worship the Apis image to the complete exclusion of God.

"When Aaron saw this, he built an altar in front of the calf and announced, 'Tomorrow there will be a festival to the Lord'" (Exodus 32:5).

"The next day the people rose early and sacrificed burnt offerings and presented fellowship offerings" (Exodus 32:6). These sacrifices were to the Lord—not the golden calf.

It was after this that the Israelites "got up to indulge in revelry" (Exodus 32:6).

Since the Apis was a symbol of virility and fertility,[4] the worship of it in Egypt would have included sex acts. Accordingly, the "revelry" on the part of the Israelites seems to imply "fornicating and adulterous intercourse."[5]

WHICH COMMANDMENT?

What should we conclude about this?

Theologian John J. Davis wrote, "The people were weary of waiting for Moses. They wanted to resume their journey to the Promised Land with a visible god at their head to inspire them with confidence and courage."[6]

The idea of a visible god in the form of the golden calf is in violation of the Second Commandment: "You shall not make for yourself an idol in the form of anything above or on the earth beneath or in the waters below. You shall not bow down to them and worship them…" (Exodus 20:4-5).

So were they guilty of violating the First or Second Commandment? Both, it seems to me.

The bottom line, however, is that "the Israelites had tragically fallen prey to cultural influences... God's people were unwittingly associating their God with the gods of the nations."[7]

The golden calf is an example of how people carry their past cultures into their worship of God as they attempt to leave their idols behind.

Meanwhile, back on top of Mount Sinai, "The Lord said to Moses, 'Go down, because your people, whom you brought up out of Egypt, have become corrupt. They have been quick to turn away from what I commanded them…'" (Exodus 32:7-8).

Moses started back down the mountain carrying two tablets of stone that "were the work of God; the writing was the writing of God, engraved on the tablets" (Exodus 32:16). When Moses "saw the calf and the dancing, his anger burned and he threw the tablets out of his hands, breaking them to pieces at the foot of the mountain" (Exodus 32:19).

As a result of their sins, 3,000 people died; others were struck with a plague, and the Lord would have destroyed Aaron except for the prayerful intervention of Moses (Deuteronomy 9:20). As for the golden calf itself, Moses burned it, ground it up, and made the

Israelites drink the water containing it.

According to Clarke's Commentary, "The Jews have a metaphorical saying, apparently founded on this text: 'No affliction has ever happened to Israel in which there was not some particle of the dust of the golden calf.'"[8]

NEW WORD, OLD BEHAVIOR

It is safe to say that the Jews don't have an exclusive franchise on golden calf dust negatively impacting their lives. Christians, too, are damaged spiritually by it as we (1) seek to follow visible gods and (2) worship God and god simultaneously, which is known as syncretism.

This word, syncretism, puts a label on something already familiar to us. Earlier, we saw that when still in Egypt, the Israelites worshipped Egyptian deities while praying to the Lord God for deliverance from slavery. I then observed that like them, I'd had my feet in opposing camps by visiting strip clubs and using pornography after returning to church.

Originally a political term, "syncretism" was used to describe the joining together of rival Greek forces on the Isle of Crete in opposition to a common enemy.[9] It now refers to "the practice of bringing together two or more distinct sets of beliefs to create an entirely new one."[10]

This may include combining aspects of two cultures, such as Mexican food in Texas being called "Tex-Mex."

Our concern has to do with religious syncretism, whereby "elements of one religion are assimilated into another religion resulting in a change in the fundamental tenets or nature of those religions…."[11]

For example, some Haitians combine Catholicism and voodoo. Also, Christians participating in yoga exercises or hosting such groups in their churches may or may not be aware that this practice is aimed at "yoking the practitioner to the Hindu god known as Brahman."[12]

Called "a long-standing tool of Satan to separate God from his people,"[13] syncretism occurs as Christian beliefs and practices are altered to "blend with those of the dominant culture," according to Dr. Gailyn Van Rheenen. As a result, "Christianity loses its distinctive nature and speaks with a voice reflective of its culture as its adherents take on the major cultural assumptions of their society."[14]

Van Rheenen gave the following example of syncretism that occurs when ethical theism accommodates modernism:

> *Christians acknowledge God and desire to be faithful to him. They believe that God sent Jesus to die for them and live with hope that they will ultimately live with God in heaven. At the same time they have a great belief in human abilities through science to solve all human problems... Christians often seek medicine and therapy for illness without relying on the Great Physician. In other words, prayer and healing are divorced as if God has little to do with life... This can lead to the belief that humanity, with its scientific understanding, is self-sufficient, able to handle all obstacles in life, and does not need God.*[15]

How has this form of syncretism emerged in your life?

SEX, SIN, AND SYNCRETISM

We saw that after the golden calf was formed, the Israelites worshipped God and then at least some of them engaged in an orgy. On this subject, God told the children of Israel through Moses, "You must not do as they do in Egypt, where you used to live, and you must not do as they do in the land of Canaan, where I am bringing you" (Leviticus 18:3). Canaan was the Promised Land.

The ancient Egyptians approved of homosexuality, prostitution, incest, sex before marriage, and abortion, according to writer Caroline Seawright, "The gods themselves were earthly enough to copulate. The Egyptians even believed in sex in the afterlife,"[16] wrote Seawright.

Sex practices in Canaan which were forbidden by God's people included incest, homosexuality, bestiality, and the sacrifice of their children to a sex god (Leviticus 18:6-23).

Worshipping God while maintaining sexual mores defined by a land-of-slavery culture is a prime example of syncretism.

My own syncretism with sex started when someone donated a bunch of *Playboy* magazines to the Boy Scout paper drive. Then from time to time, I would find magazines featuring naked women on the side of the road after they'd apparently been tossed out of cars by leering litterbugs.

The pictures went "live" when I was 16. A friend and I caught a bus to downtown Detroit to attend the early afternoon show at the Empress Burlesque on Woodward Avenue. It cost one dollar to enter an old, long, and narrow theater that smelled like roach spray. You were supposed to be 18 to get in, but they never checked IDs.

We took our seats, and a man's voice speaking into a microphone from off-stage announced, "Moving right along with the show, the lovely Barbara. Give her a hand, gentlemen." There was a smattering of applause as she stepped onstage and strutted her stuff to the sound of Roy Orbison's "Candy Man."

When Barbara started stripping, I started shaking. Why, I wasn't sure, but I can say that the forbidden fruit was looking pretty good.

After that, my buddies and I were regular patrons of the Empress and two similar venues in downtown Detroit along with a smut-showing "art theater" in the suburbs.

While a lot of people were mourning and crying just hours after the assassination of President John F. Kennedy, I was lusting over smutty movies at the art theater with some high school buddies. Coincidentally, a friend from church was there with some friends from his high school.

In the land of slavery, it was common for a single guy such as myself to go to bed with a woman on the first or second date. I knew this had to change after returning to church, and it did.

What didn't change completely, though, was my use of pornography. It was no longer non-stop, but it continued to surface from time to time.

At some point, I realized that I was much more apt to turn to pornography if I was discouraged or felt rejected. This let me know that it had drug-like effects and was very addictive.

Sometimes, though, I justified viewing porn on the basis of being single. As it turns out, men who use porn before they are married will find themselves looking at it again, often before the honeymoon is over. It then steals from the intimacy enjoyed between husband and wife to which they had looked forward.

Thankfully, I did not bring a porn habit into my marriage.

Four things have worked toward all but removing pornography in my life:

1. Prayer and ongoing spiritual growth helped me to see that pornography separates me from God.
2. Seeking God's guidance and help.
3. Seeing the devastating effects of sex addiction in the life of a friend some two decades ago and having observed many similar situations in the years since.
4. Attending a weekly men's accountability group. If I fall short—and it is so easy with the advent of the internet—I know that I'll have to confess to these men the following week.

The title of a book written by Stephen Arterburn, Fred Stoeker, and Mike Yorkey describes the pervasiveness of this problem, *Every Man's Battle*. The subtitle hints at the solution: *Winning the War on Sexual Temptation One Victory at a Time*.

Just as I go day by day or even moment by moment without using alcohol or nicotine, I attempt to apply the same idea to temptations regarding pornography with extra on-the-spot prayers.

I'm sure you noticed it, but in case you didn't: My statement about having pornography removed from my life contained the words "all but." I added those words a few days after writing this chapter because of an e-mail I received. It looked innocent enough from the outside but that belied what was inside. Included were several pictures of the same young woman, and I looked at all of them. Twice. Then I deleted the e-mail after about 45 seconds.

Days later, the images continued to appear in my head, and

they were accompanied by a desire to see them again. I confessed this to our Thursday night group. And in the future, messages from that source will be screened carefully.

Of course, there are many other types of syncretism that will draw us back toward the land of slavery.

Name some forms of syncretism that have been a part of your Christian walk.

CHAPTER THIRTEEN

Who Me? Certainly Not.

What's the best way to avoid taking responsibility for your own misguided actions? Blame someone else.

That's exactly what Aaron did for his part in the golden calf debacle.

Coming down from the mountain, Moses asked Aaron, "What did these people do to you, that you led them into such great sin?" (Exodus 32:21)

Aaron's answer contains two examples of finger-pointing, each abounding with failure to take responsibility for his own actions.

1. "You know how prone these people are to evil" (Exodus 32:22).

Following Aaron's faulty reasoning, if the people were not so evil, he wouldn't have done this. Thus, it was their fault. The fact remains, though, that Aaron had asked them for the gold to make the calf.

2. "So I told them, 'Whoever has any gold jewelry, take it off.' Then they gave me the gold, and I threw it into the fire, and out came this calf" (Exodus 32:24).

With the evidence standing there right in front of them, Aaron couldn't deny the existence of the idol. So he did the next worst thing. He said the calf had somehow come together on its own, an excuse one might expect from a four year old.

If this matter had not been so serious, Moses might have burst out laughing.

Aaron was not the first one to fall into the ploy of finger-pointing. It is a sorry trend nearly as old as sin itself because it first occurred in the Garden of Eden.

Adam and Eve had just eaten the forbidden fruit, realized they were naked, and tried to hide from God. God called out to Adam, "Where are you?" (Genesis 3:9)

Adam replied, "I heard you in the garden, and I was afraid because I was naked; so I hid" (Genesis 3:10).

God responded, "Who told you that you were naked? Have you eaten from that tree I commanded you not to eat from?" (Genesis 3:11)

Based on this question, Adam was given the opportunity to confess his failure, repent, and ask for God's mercy, but he didn't. Instead, he started finger-pointing.

"The *woman* you put here with me—she gave me some fruit from the tree, and I ate it" (Genesis 3:12, emphasis mine).

To take the heat off himself, Adam first blamed "the woman."

FACT: After the woman had eaten the fruit, "She also gave

some to her husband, who was with her, and he ate it" (Genesis 3:6). Apparently, Adam stood there watching his wife's conversation with Satan and never opened his mouth until it came time to eat the forbidden fruit. Based on Adam's response, you might think she'd force-fed him.

Next, Adam pointed his finger at God. "The woman *you* put here..." (Genesis 3:12, emphasis mine).

FACT: All of a sudden, Adam tried to make God the villain for creating Eve. This belies Adam's initial reaction to her. "This is now bone of my bones and flesh of my flesh" (Genesis 2:23).

Prior to Eve's creation, the garden had included plants, animals and Adam as the sole human. His "This is now..." statement indicates his immediate recognition of a new and special relationship. "She was in her person and in her mind every way suitable to be his companion," according to Adam Clarke's commentary.[1]

After Adam's version of the blame-game, the focus switched to Eve. "Then the Lord God said to the woman, 'What is this you have done?'" (Genesis 3:13)

Eve, too, was given the opportunity to repent but did not. Instead, she pointed her finger at Satan. "The serpent deceived me, and I ate" (Genesis 3:13).

If God had created her as a robot, Eve would have had no freedom of choice; someone or something else would have made her decisions for her in the same manner that a puppet's actions are determined by the one pulling the strings.

Eve's answer to God's question reminds me of a television documentary on obesity that featured a half-ton man unable to move from his bed. Here's how he explained his problem: "What do you expect? There are so many advertisements for food on television." Following this logic, anyone who watches television should also weigh a thousand pounds.

God had given Adam and Eve freedom of choice (Genesis 2:16), the very same as He gives us. We are not powerless over the things we see or hear.

Here is the bottom line on finger-pointing: It includes changing the facts to conform with our own lie as we blame both God and other people for our own actions. It is a means of avoiding personal responsibility for our own failings while we continue in denial with self-destructive, slave-world behavior.

Is it crystal clear why Satan would champion finger-pointing?

How have you been guilty of attempting to avoid taking personal responsibility for your own actions by finger-pointing at other people? At God?

If you continually look at the children of Israel with a "tsk-tsk" attitude and never see how you are similar to them, how is that an example of finger-pointing?

MY PARENTS FAULT?

I've already mentioned my anxieties and the phobia about driving any considerable distance in my car. For some reason, I was embarrassed about having these problems, and the few people I did manage to tell did not understand.

When I'd been sober for about a decade, I saw a television documentary about agoraphobia. It finally allowed me to put a label on the irrational thought processes from which I'd suffered. The definition of agoraphobia below pretty well sums up what was going on with me.

> *An anxiety disorder defined as a morbid fear of having a panic attack or panic-like symptoms in a situation that is perceived to be difficult (or embarrassing) from which to escape. These situations can include, but are not limited to wide-open spaces, crowds, or uncontrolled social conditions... In severe cases, the sufferer may become confined to his or her home, unable to leave their safe haven.*[2]

As a result of this problem, I started seeing a psychologist around my 24th birthday. I also expressed concern to him about my heavy alcohol consumption. He assured me that my drinking would moderate and these fears would disappear once he and I got to the root of my problems.

Exactly what lay at this root? According to him, it had to do with growing up in a dysfunctional home.

I bought into this slave-world lie because it allowed me to continue clinging to the idol of alcohol while waiting for the psychologist to take away my problems.

In what ways have you bought into this same lie?

In the meantime, the psychologist and I drank together on a couple of occasions. He also encouraged me to smoke marijuana, advice I didn't take because I'd already tried it and didn't like the effects.

During my frequent drunken stupors, I would stew in anger over the way my parents had failed me. I called to tell them what a poor job they had done.

Following in the tradition of Adam, my greatest grandfather, I also blamed God for the problems resulting from my wrong choices. Here is my deluded reasoning: If only I had not been exposed to ideas about God and religion, I would not have been burdened by what I considered Victorian-era guilt. This would have allowed me to throw myself even more whole-heartedly into a life of partying and promiscuity.

It seemed obvious to me that my drinking associates were not impacted by such guilt nor were they suffering from anxieties.

Continuing in psychological counseling for the next couple of years, my mental state worsened as my episodes of drunkenness increased until I finally entered the mental hospital.

As a patient there, I visited a psychiatrist every other day. He never inquired about my alcohol consumption.

After discussions with my fellow patient, Ron, about the down sides of drinking, I asked the psychiatrist if I might be an alcoholic. "It's possible," he replied. That was about as far as it went.

Neither the psychologist nor psychiatrist ever mentioned the fact that drunkenness is a sin. The Bible warns, "Do not get drunk on wine which leads to debauchery" (Ephesians 5:18). Drunkenness also is listed as an "act of the sinful nature" (Galatians 5:20) with a warning "that those who live like this will not inherit the kingdom of God" (Galatians 5:21).

Rather than treating the cause of my problems (alcohol consumption), the psychologist attempted to treat the symptoms which manifested themselves as agoraphobia. Many people undoubtedly have this disorder without drinking. For me, though, it started when I was boozing heavily after college graduation and gradually diminished over a period of time after I got sober.

The psychologist I visited had earned his Ph.D. from the University of Michigan, a prestigious institution of higher learning. As you would find at most universities, the psychology program there was and is steeped in modernism. Undoubtedly, post-modern thought has been seeping into these programs more recently.

Do I blame the psychologist for misguidance? No, I can only blame myself for turning my back on God and putting my faith in someone whom I knew to be an atheist.

MORE SYNCRETISM

Pop psychology today emanates from the media, some church pulpits, and many other sources. Our culture is saturated with it.

A problem that may not be readily apparent to Christians is that psychology and religion are "competing faiths," according to Dr. William Kirk Kilpatrick. "If you seriously hold to one set of values," he writes, "you will logically have to reject the other."[3]

He explained how this form of syncretism came to fruition in his own life:

> *Religion and psychology had become nearly indistinguishable for me. Freud and the church fathers, faith in God and faith in human potential, revelation and self-revelation—all slid together in an easy companionship. As for God, He began to take shape in my mind along the lines of a friendly counselor of the nondirective school. I never balked at doing His will. His will always coincided with my own.*[4]

Dr. Gary L. Almy elaborates below on the impact of psychology in our culture while encapsulating "the gospel" espoused by the psychologist I visited.

> *The vast majority of both non-Christians and professing Christians believe that we humans are essentially born innocent and basically good, and that we would all be leading lives of health and happiness, at our full potential, if only a bad environment had not intervened. If I am not healthy, happy, and functioning at an optimal level, then the responsibility lies outside of me. My misery and general lack of success must be due to my parents, my family, the neighborhood, the culture, the environment.*[5]

As a result, "Countless Christians worry more about losing their self-esteem than about losing their souls,"[6] writes psychology professor Paul Vitz.

EXAMINE THE ROOTS

"Most people do not even think twice about the origin of some of the psychological ideas they take for granted,"[7] wrote Martin and Deidre Bobgan in their book, *Psycho Heresy: The Psychological Seduction of Christianity*.

To give you an idea of these origins, let's take a brief look at some individuals who have had the greatest impact on psychology as we know it today.

Sigmund Freud (1856-1939), the "father of psychoanalysis," was openly hostile to Christianity and assumed "that people could solve their own problems without the help of God or any other supernatural source."[8]

Among Freud's first contributions to the medical world was an 1884 research article titled *Uber Coca* (On Cocaine), a then-legal drug to which he became addicted and called "his most gorgeous excitement."[9]

Freud also believed that cigars made him more creative and productive. He never gave up smoking them despite being diagnosed with oral cancer in 1923. Freud endured more than 30 surgeries for his cancer, and it finally got to the point where he used prostheses to talk and eat.[10]

In the end, Freud was euthanized at his own request by Dr. Max Schur, who administered a giant dose of morphine.[11]

Although many of his ideas have been discredited and few today would claim Freudian roots...

> *...present day psychologists still follow many of his theories and use his jargon. Freud created suspicion toward parents and reduced the root of many problems to childhood traumas. This search in the past for causes is a major theme in psychology today.*[12]

Others having the greatest influence on what has been considered the "truth" of psychology include Carl Jung, Carl Rogers, Arthur Janov, Albert Ellis, Alfred Adler, Eric Berne, Erich Fromm and Abraham Maslow. None were Christians, and some shared Freud's anti-religious views.[13]

According to a Christian critique on psychology,

> *men like Freud and Jung eroded confidence in Christianity and established systems in direct opposition to the Word of God. Occultism, atheism, and antagonism towards Christianity were disguised by psychological, scientific-sounding language.*[14]

ANOTHER IDOL

I was immersed into psychological thinking via college classes, numerous books, many sessions with the psychologist, and undoubtedly, other ways that I do not remember. As a result, psychological thinking was an idol I carried with me on my trip toward the Promised Land.

In prayer, I sometimes explained myself to God in psychological terms. There's a good chance that even today, I carry around assumptions of "truth" that are based on psychology and am not even aware of them.

Even if you have never been exposed personally to psychological theory as a part of your education or as a part of counseling, there's a good chance that you, too, are impacted because of its pervasiveness in our culture.

Are you, too, carrying this cultural idol?

If yes, how has it manifested itself in your life?

If no, is it possible that you are carrying it but are not aware of it?

For a concise and very readable account on how Christianity and psychology are diametrically opposed, see the booklet by Martha Peace, *Psychologized Man*, Focus Publishing, Bemidji, MN.

But, Don, you may be thinking, the psychologist you visited was an atheist. What about Christian psychology?

During the last two to three decades, several Christian experts have written, in effect, that the notion of Christian psychology is an oxymoron. Even today, there is no consensus as to what constitutes Christian psychology. (For example, see Eric L. Johnson, editor, *Psychology & Christianity: Five Views, 2nd Edition*, Intervarsity Press, Downers Grove, IL, 2010.)

Many well-meaning counselors are not even aware of what lies at the roots of the theories they embrace. "Numerous are the examples of Christian psychologists who are ordained ministers. They begin with a desire to Christianize psychology and end up psychologizing Christianity."[15]

Before concluding this section, it is important to add this: There are any number of ways that Christian people—even those trying their very best—end up in mental turmoil with the need of professional help. Where are they to turn?

Author David M. Tyler provided an answer.

> *Ungodliness leads to unrighteousness which leads to guilt, depression, anxiety, fear, shame, etc. For counseling to be truly Biblical in nature and please God, it must be directed at changing the heart and not merely modifying behavior.*[16]

On the topic of choosing the right counselor, I talked with a long-time friend, Dr. Harold Duncan, a psycho-therapist who practices in Dallas. He does not refer to himself as a Christian psychologist, per se. According to him, that may mean anything from a counselor who prays with you to one who does not cuss. Rather, he calls himself a Christian who works as a psychologist.

How do Christians in need of counseling find the right person to help them? Dr. Duncan recommends selecting a counselor who believes Satan is a literal being and the source of evil. This counselor sees a part of his/her role as helping patients uncover satanic lies to which they subscribe and may not even be aware of them.

How does one find such an individual? Dr. Duncan suggests taking the time to interview some possible candidates to discover the basis of their faith and how it impacts the way they help patients. Of course, recommendations from fellow Christians also may be helpful.

THE RIGHT LABEL

I foundered for several years focusing on the symptoms of my problems. The recovery group helped me to put the right label on what ailed me: alcohol. I admitted that I was powerless over alcohol, that my life had become unmanageable.

These measures were very proactive. As opposed to finger-pointing and waiting for a psychologist to take away my problems, the onus was on me to remember that I was an alcoholic and could not drink normally, that no human power could help me, and that God could and would if he were sought.

As God's truth sank in, I could see the folly of blaming my parents. Were they perfect? Certainly not. Only God is the perfect father. But they were very good parents who gave me a host of advantages in life, including my religious upbringing, the importance of education, and a strong work ethic. I made amends to them for the pointless and needless accusations I'd made earlier.

In our society, what sources of information are influential in guiding people to buy into "the blame-game?"

In what ways have you blamed parents or others for problems you brought on yourself?

Name some instances when putting the right label on your spiritual problem(s) guided you in moving forward.

CHAPTER FOURTEEN

The Boomerang Effect of Judging

A friend who owns a small business moved his office from a blue-collar suburb of a large metropolitan area to an extremely affluent section of the city. "Cindy," his long-time administrative assistant and a native of the original community, quit a few weeks later.

"Was the drive too far for her?" I inquired about the 10-mile difference.

"No," he replied. "Cindy wasn't comfortable in our new setting. When she walked in this neighborhood and went to the local restaurants for lunch, she thought people were looking down on her."

A sad scenario, isn't it? This woman was a victim of judging because other people thought they were better than she was based on differences in social class and income—at least that's the way Cindy perceived it.

She was correct about being a victim of judging. She was not accurate, however, as to who was doing the judging. Cindy actually was a victim of her own judging.

In order for Cindy to conclude accurately that other people thought they were better than she was, she would have had to know something only God could know—namely, the thoughts of people around her.

She also assumed that others had both the motivation and ability to determine her income and social class by simply looking at her. Then by judging that others thought she was inferior, Cindy demonstrated her own materialism.

Who was hurt by all of this? She was.

Judging is often tied to finger-pointing, the topic of the last chapter. Here's what Jesus said of this relationship:

> *Do not judge, or you too will be judged. For in the same way you judge others, you will be judged... Why do you look at the speck of sawdust in your brother's eye and pay no attention to the plank in your own eye? How can you say to your brother, "Let me take the speck out of your eye," when all the time there is a plank in your own eye? You hypocrite, first take the plank out of your own eye, and then you will see clearly to remove the speck from your brother's eye (Matthew 7:1-5).*

Finger-pointing is a means of avoiding self-examination by looking at the faults of others, while the detrimental type of judging we're discussing includes making inferences about others with information only God could possess. This information often includes assumptions about another person's motives.

Finger-pointing and judging merge because judgments usually reflect our own shortcomings.

Here are some incidents of judging on the part of the children of Israel:

When they were camped by the Red Sea and Pharaoh's army was closing in, the Israelites pointed their fingers at Moses and stated, "Was it because there were no graves in Egypt that you brought us to the desert to die?" (Exodus 14:11)

In their stress, they incorrectly judged Moses's reason for taking them out of slavery. Since it already had been established that Moses was speaking to them on behalf of the Almighty, the Israelites simultaneously judged God.

Just before God started providing manna about six weeks later, the children of Israel judged the motives of God, Moses, and Aaron by saying, "You have brought us out into this desert to starve this entire assembly to death" (Exodus 16:3).

The same thing happened later when the Israelites were camped at Rephidim where there was no water. Pointing fingers at Moses, they stated, "Why did you bring us up out of Egypt to make us and our children and livestock die of thirst?" (Exodus 17:3)

If they'd only looked at their recent past, they would have seen that God had provided safe crossing through the Red Sea, water at both Marah and Elim, and manna in the Desert of Sin.

As with finger-pointing, there is nothing new about judging. Satan judged God as a part of his temptation to Eve. "For God knows that when you eat of it your eyes will be opened, and you will be like God, knowing good and evil" (Genesis 3:5).

This statement from the epitome of evil contains two separate incidents of judging.

1. "For God knows" is a lie and a form of judging because it

assumes that the devil knows the mind of God. (If he really did, he would be God.)

2. The devil also judged God's motives because as a part of his native language (lies), he makes it sound like God's motivation for the prohibition against eating the forbidden fruit was to keep Eve from having a wonderful eye-opening experience.

Name some ways that you have judged wrongly the motivations of others. How have you judged the motivations of God?

A COMPARISON THAT HURTS US

Cindy made a judgment by what is referred to as comparing her insides to other people's outsides. The Psalmist Asaph did the same thing, and so have I.

Here's what Asaph wrote,

> *For I envied the arrogant when I saw the prosperity of the wicked. They have no struggles; their bodies are healthy and strong. They are free from the burdens common to man; they are not plagued by human ills (Psalm 73:3-5).*

On the basis of his perspective distorted by envy, Asaph judged arrogant people as being without problems. Of course, only God knew whether these individuals were "healthy and strong," if they were "free from the burdens common to man," and "not plagued by human ills."

When he stopped pointing his finger at them and judged himself, Asaph concluded, "When my heart was grieved and my spirit embittered, I was senseless and ignorant; I was a brute beast before you" (Psalm 73:21-22).

Recall my Corvette. A part of what led me to elevate this car to idol status was because in my envy and twisted logic, I had judged Corvette owners to be superior to me.

Also as mentioned earlier, I blamed God for the guilt I experienced while drinking and thought I was the only one having anxieties and questioning my standards of morality. As it turned out, a young woman in that drinking crowd was having similar thoughts about her own standards.

This woman was drunk just about every time I saw her. Shortly after I stopped drinking and attending raucous parties, I was told that she showed up at one of these gatherings and followed her usual custom of drinking herself into oblivion. In this condition, she spewed vomit all over herself. "Robert," mentioned earlier, told me that he and some others guys decided to "help" her by taking off all her clothes and giving her a shower.

A few days later she went back to the party house and told them calmly that with her religious upbringing, her recent lifestyle did not represent the kind of person she wished to be. She then followed her words with actions, the same as I had.

Thinking that I was the only one experiencing guilt due to my lifestyle served simply to increase my feelings of isolation.

In what ways have you judged the outsides of others by your insides? How has this been to your detriment?

JESUS WAS JUDGED

There are plenty of examples in the Bible of Jesus being judged wrongly by His enemies. More remarkable, however, is the fact that on at least three occasions detailed below, He also was judged by His friends and family. Each instance contains an accusation that could not have been further from the truth.

1. Jesus slept on a cushion in the stern of a boat as He and His disciples crossed the Sea of Galilee. "A furious squall came up, and the waves broke over the boat, so that it was nearly swamped" (Mark 4:37). Waking Him, the disciples exclaimed, "Teacher, don't you care if we drown?" (Mark 4:38)

Jesus was judged as not caring whether they died. Similar accusations pointed at God, Moses, and Aaron, also created by stress, were cited earlier as coming from the children of Israel.

Have you ever judged the Lord as not caring about you?

2. Jesus visited the home of sisters, Mary and Martha. Mary sat at Jesus's feet listening to His words. "But Martha was distracted by all the preparations that had to be made. She came to him and asked, 'Lord, don't you care that my sister has left me to do the work by myself? Tell her to help me'" (Luke 10:40).

Martha's judging was a product of her self-induced stress. In the words of Jesus, she was "worried and upset about many things" (Luke 10:41) resulting in her misplaced priorities. As Jesus told her, "Only one thing is needed. Mary has chosen what is better, and it will not be taken away from her" (Luke 10:41).

Have you created stress in your own life due to illusions of martyrdom?

In what way did it cause you to judge the people around you? To judge the Lord?

3. Jesus was conducting His work in Galilee, keeping a distance from Judea because the Jews there were waiting to kill Him. With the Jewish Feast of the Tabernacles approaching, His brothers approached Him, "You ought to leave here and go to Judea, so that your disciples may see the miracles you do. No one who wants to become a public figure acts in secret" (John 7:4).

In essence, they judged Jesus of wishing to become a big shot. According to the Apostle John, their motive had to do with their own disbelief in His divinity (John 7:5).

In what way have you similarly judged family members or others?

JUDGING FROM A GUILTY KING

King David provided a classic example of the way finger-pointing is related to judging.

While his army was off fighting a war, David stayed home and had a one-night stand with his neighbor Bathsheba, getting her pregnant. She was the wife of one of his bravest soldiers, Uriah the Hittite.

As part of an attempted cover-up, David had Uriah called in from the battlefield with hopes that Uriah would have relations with his wife and believe the baby was his. When this failed, David sent a note to his general ordering him to put Uriah into a position where he would be killed. This ploy worked, and David then married Bathsheba.

Once called a man after God's own heart (I Samuel 13:14), David was in denial. The Lord sent the prophet Nathan to do an intervention. Nathan started this meeting by telling David the following story.

There were two men in the same city—one rich, the other poor. The rich man had huge flocks of sheep, herds of cattle. The poor man had nothing but one little female lamb, which he had bought and raised. It grew up with him and his children as a member of the family. It ate off his plate and drank from his cup and slept on his bed. It was like a daughter to him.

One day a traveler dropped in on the rich man. He was too stingy to take an animal from his own herds or flocks to make a meal for his visitor, so he took the poor man's lamb and prepared a meal to set before his guest (II Samuel 12:1-4, The Message).

Hearing this story, David "burned with anger" (II Samuel 12:5). This was tied to finger-pointing. David was looking at the faults of the rich man from Nathan's story. Using Jesus's terms from Matthew 7:3-5, David focused on a speck in the eye of the rich man (killing an animal) in comparison to the plank in David's eye (having sex with another man's wife and then having him killed) which obstructed his perspective.

This phenomenon with the speck and the plank is referred to as "You spot it, you've got it." It also is known as "If you've got one finger pointed in accusation at someone else, you've got three pointed back at yourself," and "It takes one to know one." As painful as this may be, if we pay attention to the specks in the eyes of others we find so upsetting, it will tell us a lot about ourselves.

Name some ways that your finger-pointing has resulted from the plank in your eye.

What did it take for you to recognize your fault?

Concluding his finger-pointing, David judged the situation. "As surely as the Lord lives, the man who did this deserves to die" (II Samuel 12:5). David's judgment of capital punishment was much more severe than that required by the law of Moses, which included paying back four sheep for the one stolen (Exodus 22:1). While David did go on to cite what would be required under the old law, the death sentence he pronounced is actually what *he* deserved under that same law (Numbers 35:30).

Then the truth came out. "You are the man!" Nathan told David.

You can picture David sitting there with his mouth wide open in surprise as Nathan then pronounced David's guilt and spelled out the consequences of his sin. (See II Samuel 12:8-12.)

Finally coming out of denial and recognizing God's truth, David confessed, "I have sinned against the Lord" (II Samuel 12:13).

What has it taken for you to come out of denial in regard to judging that follows finger-pointing?

IDEAS OF DEITY

When we judge others, we assume things about ourselves:

1. We are completely objective and not at all influenced by bias, favoritism or any manifestation of ego.
2. We do not have any planks or even specks in our own eyes that obscure the way we view the world.
3. We are always correct.
4. We have kept a complete record of the thoughts and actions of those around us and know how these things affect everyone else.

Undoubtedly, you noticed that the above-listed assumptions are all characteristics of God, and as such, judging results from slave-world, Satan-championed thinking.

Paul wrote, "Judge nothing before the appointed time; wait till the Lord comes. He will bring to light what is hidden in darkness and will expose the motives of men's hearts. At that time each will receive his praise from God" (I Corinthians 4:5).

CHAPTER FIFTEEN

A Hot Tamale Hunger

Thinking in terms of alcohol flowing the most freely, what would you consider to be the number one party night of any particular year?

Some might argue for the Super Bowl, but New Year's Eve still reigns supreme in that category based on my past experience. This night is long known for overindulgence. As testimony to that, on December 31 of each year, the media usually report the best cures for a hangover.

Of course, in my circle of friends, there was always a big party planned for that night, and it was an unspoken assumption that everyone would get ripped.

Two New Year's Eves stick out in my mind.

One of them was when my sister and I hosted a get-together at our house when she was 20 and I was 21. We'd both attended plenty of raucous parties at the respective state universities we attended, and we had no reason to expect the celebration at our house to be anything different.

Our parents, however, had no such expectation. They did not know our "norm" for parties, and I can guarantee that their social gatherings were a lot different. They usually didn't drink at all, but if they did, it was with extreme moderation. My mother's favorite saying about beer was, "As far as I'm concerned you can pour it back into the horse."

When mom and dad returned home from the party they'd attended about 12:30 a.m., our party was just getting warmed up. They parked in the garage and walked toward the front door. They immediately heard some laughter.

Continuing in that direction, they encountered the source of the merriment: a female party-goer who'd overindulged and fallen off the front porch into a shrub. Her legs were sticking up in the air, and she was unable to extract herself. Of course, they helped her.

That greeting was just a preview of what they found when they stepped inside.

Hearing their thoughts on the subject the following day, my sister and I each wondered why they should be so upset. Of course, we subsequently came to understand.

Fast-forward to the New Year's Eve that would usher in the year 1975. It was nearly 14 months since my last drink. A year earlier with only seven weeks of sobriety, I was still straddling the fence and had gone to a party with old drinking friends but hadn't imbibed myself. In the 12 months since then, however, I'd mostly lost track of that old party crowd.

Where would I spend New Year's Eve?

MISDIRECTED APPETITES

After about two years in the wilderness, the children of Israel set up camp at a place that was subsequently called Kibroth Hattaavah, which means Graves of the Craving.[1] Doesn't exactly sound like a vacation get-away, does it?

Just prior to arriving at that location, the Israelites had done a lot of whining that displeased the Lord and received a stern warning. "Fire from the Lord burned among them and consumed some of the outskirts of the camp" (Numbers 11:1). The Israelites sought help from Moses, who prayed for them. The fire then subsided.

You'd think they might have heeded the warning, but they didn't.

Here's what happened next:

> *The rabble with them began to crave other food, and again the Israelites started wailing and said, "If only we had meat to eat! We remember the fish we ate in Egypt at no cost—also the cucumbers, melons, leeks, onions and garlic. But now we have lost our appetite; we never see anything but this manna!" (Numbers 11:4-6)*

Originally, not everyone craved meat, only "the rabble," translated as "riffraff" in *The Message*, and "mixt multitude" in the King James. Biblical scholars say these people, first identified in Exodus 12:38, were non-Israelite tag-alongs with little or no desire to serve the Lord.[2] Their sentiments quickly spread to the Israelites, a reminder about the possible negative effects of our associates (I Corinthians 15:33).

On the surface at least, what was said about the fish being free in Egypt was factual. Fish could be caught in the Nile or in the numerous canals running from it. Missed in this observation, however, is that in order to get free fish, people had to live in a land where they weren't free.

This is the devil's bargain.

Note that the craving was not due to hunger. Rather, it was a dietary preference for the meat and spicy stuff that was available in the land of slavery as opposed to God-supplied manna.

Craving is defined as "an abnormal or excessive desire, as for a food or drug."[3] To act on a craving for something from the land of slavery is to believe a lie.

God viewed their craving and whining as rejection of Him (Numbers 11:20).

Writing about this episode in *The Land Between*, Jeff Manion observed, "They were not simply rejecting the food; they were rejecting their God."[4] They were saying, in essence, "We were better off without you as our rescuer, we were better off without your presence, we were better off as slaves, we would have had a better life living among the gods of Egypt."[5]

Through Moses, here is God's response to the craving for Egyptian food:

> *Tell the people, consecrate yourselves. Get ready for tomorrow when you're going to eat meat... And it's not just for a day that you'll eat meat, and not two days, or five or ten or twenty, but for a whole month. You're going to eat meat until it's coming out your nostrils. You're going to be so sick of meat that you'll throw up at the mere mention of it* (Numbers 11:18-20, *The Message*).

Could this warning be any more simple? Today, someone might ask, "What part of projectile vomiting do you not understand?"

The next day, a wind blew in a huge flock of quail that had crossed the sea. These birds piled up three feet in camp and a day's walk in every direction from the camp. The least gathered by anyone filled 60 bushels.

What happened next reminds me of an experiment involving cocaine and lab animals. Those allowed to self-administer cocaine every 50 seconds all died within 30 days. Monkeys allowed to take cocaine every 10 seconds all died within five days.

But you don't have to be an animal to do something like this. You could just act like one.

For example, a man told me how he caught hepatitis C from using a needle to inject drugs into his arm after it had just been used by another drug addict. Despite knowing the dangers of sharing a needle and even knowing how to sterilize one, he didn't take the one minute it would take to do it.

Craving for the drug trumped his logic. He didn't do this out of ignorance. He was a college graduate, a former student of mine.

Have you ever done anything with full knowledge that it was against God's will and would end up being bad for you?

"While the meat was still between their teeth and before it could be consumed, the Lord... struck them with a severe plague" (Numbers 11:33). Then "they buried the people who had craved other food" (Numbers 11:34).

Those free fish in Egypt really aren't free. The price you pay for them may include your life—your own soul, even.

PLAIN-JANE FOOD

While I have never tasted manna, I can't imagine it is anything like Cajun food, a meat-lover's pizza with double anchovies, or blazing-hot buzzard-meat chili concocted at a Texas cook-off.

"Manna was like coriander seed and looked like resin. The people… cooked it in a pot or made it into cakes. And it tasted like something made with olive oil" (Numbers 11:7).

Living in the land of slavery is a lot spicier than life on the way to the Promised Land. Starting in my late teens, I sought out a thrill-a-minute spice diet.

It was a roller-coaster existence—exhilarating at first— gradually changing so there were few high points and a whole lot of lows. Finally, there were no highs, and the low points turned to despair; suicide seemed the only way out.

The God-led journey does not include all those ups and downs, and it leads toward a quieter life with contentment coming from the inside out. The promise is a better life now and eternity with our Creator.

Despite knowing this, the spice continues to beckon, usually in different forms than earlier. For me, these include the emotions generated by listening to political talk radio, swings in the stock market, investments in high-risk ventures, or juicy gossip.

What was your past preference for spice? What is it today?

Slave-world thinking involves a series of potential payouts perceived to be huge. There is an adrenalin rush when the literal or figurative horse on which we bet is dashing down the home stretch in a close race. If it wins, there is a moment of elation before we select a horse in the next race, pick up our winnings, and bet again. If it loses, there is a moment of desolation before we select a horse in the next race, take some money from our wallets, and bet again.

In the above scenario, the real payout is not in the outcome of the race but in the race itself. Although the people involved usually don't see it that way, their routine is like riding painted plastic horses that go up and down, round and round on a merry-go-round that digs itself deeper into the ground with each rotation.

NONE OF US VOMITED

Determining where I would go to a party on the evening of December 31, 1974, I chose manna and went to the party in the church basement.

When singing church hymns at the stroke of midnight with a lot of people I hadn't known the year before, many of them the age of my parents, I felt kind of silly. To say that this party was bland in comparison to the spice of the previous years is an understatement.

What would my old friends think if they saw me there? Had I turned into a religious nerd who was content to lead a boring and bland life?

Thankfully, these thoughts were outweighed by recalling my past slavery to alcohol, those last desperate swigs in the parking lot of the mental hospital, and that it was God who delivered me.

Surrounded by new Christian friends, I decided it was not very important what my old friends thought. I was where I needed to be, heading in the general direction of a promised land that was moving in my mind from mere theory to the assurances of a brighter future.

The change of diet was exactly what I needed.

Please pass the manna.

**In your everyday life,
how do you determine the difference between spice and manna?**

CHAPTER SIXTEEN

Well, Shut My Mouth

One Saturday when I was 11 years old, Dad took me to the Western Open golf tournament. We followed golfing legend Sam Snead around the front nine. Then we sat near the green on the 198-yard, par-three ninth hole and watched the pros hit their tee shots. For them, it was not a matter of landing on the green, but how far they would be from the pin.

That tournament, more recently known as the BMW Championship, was hosted at Plum Hollow Country Club in Southfield, Michigan, about five miles away from where we lived.

At ages 15 and 16, I worked at Plum Hollow as a caddy during the summers and observed that many golfers did not hit the green with their tee shots on the ninth hole. For those who didn't, there was a price to pay. The tee and green were separated by a deep, steep-sided gully. From the bottom of it, the green was not even visible.

Of all the golfers with whom I was associated during those two summers, one continues to stand out in my mind for what occurred on the ninth hole.

Seven of us (the other three golfers and four caddies) watched as he went into his back swing and started to bring his club head forward. Then lifting his head, he topped the ball and it dribbled down the hill. No big deal, it happened all the time. What happened next is why I remember.

He muttered, "#&#@%%$" and then yelled out, "#*@%!" We then watched in amazement as he launched his three iron in the general direction of the green. It produced a whirring noise as it sailed end over end and finally made a barely perceptible splat as it landed in a mud hole at the bottom.

The golfer stood there for a moment and then looked over at the rest of us rather sheepishly. I recall that his caddie dutifully retrieved the club from the mud, wiped it clean, and returned it to the golfer's bag.

Of course, we caddies maintained somber expressions as this scene unfolded before our eyes but recounted it with glee when we got back to the caddy shack.

I'm sorry to report that when I took up golf, I put on some similar spectacles for the same reason. During those few years I pursued golf some three decades ago, I also made some terrific shots. One time, I barely missed a hole-in-one when I rimmed the cup with my drive on a par-three hole and ended up with a six-inch putt.

Of course, anyone can be gracious after making a great golf shot, but not everyone holds his tongue after a bad one.

I was reminded of all this recently while teaching a Sunday morning Bible class at my church. Charley Johnston, one of our elders, quoted his father as saying something like this, "You can tell a lot about people by their words and actions on the golf course."

I squirmed inwardly.

"A fool gives full vent to his anger, but a wise man keeps himself under control" (Proverbs 29:11).

VARYING VOCABULARY

Jesus compared a tree and its fruit (Matthew 12:33) to observe that our words are a reflection of what's going on inside of us. "For out of the overflow of the heart the mouth speaks. The good man brings good things out of the good stored up in him, and the evil man brings evil things out of the evil stored up in him" (Matthew 12:34-35).

Our words, then, are very important indicators of whether we will stay on the road toward the Promised Land or head back toward slavery.

The biblical author James observed, "Everyone should be quick to listen, slow to speak and slow to become angry" (James 1:19).

In the same vein, he added, "With the tongue we praise our Lord and Father, and with it we curse men who have been made in God's likeness. Out of the same mouth come praise and cursing. My brothers, this should not be" (James 3:9-10).

This dualism described by James was apparent among the children of Israel from the get-go. Recall that the enslaved children of Israel listened to Moses and Aaron tell about their forthcoming deliverance, and they worshipped God (Exodus 4: 31). Then tough times came shortly thereafter when Pharaoh forced the Israelites to make bricks without straw. Suddenly, Moses and Aaron became their villains.

This was the first instance of a pattern that included praising God until a problem surfaced and then letting their mouths run amok with finger-pointing accusations and judging God and their leaders.

Following is a listing of the words coming from the children of Israel: "Cried out" (Exodus 14:10); "grumbled" (Exodus 15:24); "grumbled" (Exodus 16:2); "quarreled" (Exodus 17:2); "grumbled" (Exodus 17:3); "complained" (Numbers 11:1); "started wailing" (Numbers 11:4); "raised their voices and wept aloud" (Numbers 14:1); "grumbled" (Numbers 14:2); "grumble" (Numbers 14:36); "became insolent" (Numbers 16:1); "grumbled" (Numbers 16:41); "quarreled" (Numbers 20:3); "spoke against God and against Moses" (Numbers 21:4).

This is a pretty sorry record, but considering that these instances occurred over a period of 40 years, my performance is undoubtedly worse.

How does the record of your words compare?

AN ATTITUDE OF INGRATITUDE

The children of Israel watched as the plagues devastated the Egyptians but left them unscathed. They praised God after the miraculous parting of the Red Sea allowed them to escape while Pharaoh's pursuing army was destroyed. The Israelites also received daily assurances of God's guidance from the pillar of cloud and pillar of fire and from God-provided food six days a week.

Despite all of this, the children of Israel often reverted to a glass-is-half-empty perspective.

In short, they were not grateful for God's blessings and what came out of their mouths was simply a reflection of their ingratitude. This was evident just prior to the deadly quail feast. "Moses heard the people of every family wailing, each at the entrance to his tent" (Numbers 11:10).

On our own journeys, we have the choice of whining about what we don't have or looking to God and giving thanks for His blessings.

The importance of gratitude is expressed throughout the Bible. On one side of the coin, people known for their "godlessness and wickedness" (Romans 1:18) are described this way: "For although they knew God, they neither glorified him as God *nor gave thanks to him*, but their thinking became futile and their foolish hearts were darkened" (Romans 1: 21, emphasis mine).

Conversely, Paul's description of a Christian life includes people "overflowing with thankfulness" (Colossians 2:7).

He also wrote, "Let the peace of Christ rule in your hearts, since as members of one body you were called to peace. And be thankful" (Colossians 3:15).

Also, "Devote yourselves to prayer, being watchful and thankful" (Colossians 4:2).

I have received some good lessons in gratitude while teaching a class in the Collin County Detention Center, north of Dallas, Texas. These incarcerated men, many of them facing prison terms, have told me that they are grateful to be locked up. Jail time, they say, has taken them away from self-destructive routines and given them time to reflect on the direction of their lives. Many are ready to change.

As a part of a chain prayer before our class two days ago, several of the inmates thanked God for, among other things, waking up in the morning.

I can't remember ever thanking God for that.

Have you?

What are the signs of gratitude as you approach God in prayer?

FINGER-POINTING & THE LIE

The words we speak may reflect the influence of the evil one. Remember, he is "the father of lies" (John 8:44).

"I didn't do it," states the shoplifter caught with the stolen goods in his or her pocket. This is an obvious lie. There are also much more subtle lies.

For example, lying is a part of judging and finger-pointing discussed earlier. Look at two separate incidents among the Israelites.

After they left Egypt, the children of Israel were backed up against the Red Sea with Pharaoh's army approaching. They were described as "terrified" (Exodus 14:10). Here's what they blurted out:

Was it because there were no graves in Egypt that you brought us to the desert to die? What have you done to us by bringing us out of Egypt? Didn't we say to you in Egypt, "Leave us alone; let us serve the Egyptians? It would have been better for us to serve the Egyptians than to die in the desert!" (Exodus 14:10-12)

This statement contains at least three lies.

1. It was not true that Moses took them into the desert to die.
2. It was not true that they would have been better off serving the Egyptians in slavery.
3. There is no record that while they were still in Egypt, the Israelites had said, "Leave us alone, let us serve the Egyptians."

Six weeks into their desert journey, the Israelites complained to Moses and Aaron about food.

"If only we had died by the Lord's hand in Egypt! There we sat around pots of meat and ate all the food we wanted, but you have brought us out into this desert to starve this entire assembly to death" (Exodus 16:3).

This statement also contains at least two lies and another probable whopper.

1. They would not have been better off dead in Egypt.
2. It is not true that Moses took them out in the desert to starve them to death.
3. It is doubtful that slave life included sitting around pots of meat and eating all they wanted.

Even when stressed, we are accountable for the words that come out of our mouths.

LISTEN

After The Ten Commandments were issued, God reminded the children of Israel about staying focused on Him while giving them assurances about their remaining journey toward the Promised Land and the victories they would have once they arrived there. (See Exodus 23:20-33.)

Here's how this passage starts:

> *See, I am sending an angel ahead of you to guard you along the way and to bring you to the place I have prepared. Pay attention to him and listen to what he says... If you listen carefully to what he says and do all that I say... (Exodus 23:20-22).*

It has been said that the fact that God gave us two ears and only one mouth is an indication of the frequency in which we use them.

When I joined the recovery group, they told me, "Take the cotton out of your ears and put it in your mouth." I'm still working on that.

I could write on and on about how my mouth has gotten me into trouble, but instead, you'll find much more wisdom in the scriptures found below focusing on this very subject.

"Everyone should be quick to listen, slow to speak and slow to become angry…" (James 1:19).

"A man of knowledge uses words with restraint…" (Proverbs 17:27).

"He who answers before listening—that is his folly and his shame" (Proverbs 18:13).

"Let another praise you, and not your own mouth; someone else, and not your own lips" (Proverbs 27:2).

"If a man loudly blesses his neighbor early in the morning, it will be taken as a curse" (Proverbs 27:14).

"A gossip betrays a confidence; so avoid a man who talks too much" (Proverbs 20:19).

"Do you see a man who speaks in haste? There is more hope for a fool than for him" (Proverbs 29:20).

"A fool finds no pleasure in understanding but delights in airing his own opinions" (Proverbs 18:2).

"Even a fool is thought to be wise if he keeps silent, and discerning if he holds his tongue" (Proverbs 17:28).

Name some instances when you needed to listen rather than talk.

Why do you think James wrote, "No man can tame the tongue. It is a restless evil, full of deadly poison." (James 3:8)?

WHAT DID JESUS SAY?

A lot can be learned by reading through the Gospels to focus on the words that Jesus used. When I have done this, I discovered that He asked a lot of questions. Attempting to follow suit has made me a better teacher.

I've also discovered that asking questions has the potential to make me a better person. Why?

1. I never learn when I'm talking but have the potential to learn while listening.
2. Listening gets my mind off me.
3. Listening puts me in a position to understand what's going on with another person, and then I am more apt to be able to help that person.

Whether you believe you are a one-talent or a 10-talent person or something in between, there is a ministry you could initiate right now without any special training. It is a listening ministry.

To start, ask someone a question about him or herself. As the person replies, don't think of your own response, but listen to what the individual is saying so that you are in a better position to ask another question. Challenge yourself to see how long you can go without interjecting anything into the conversation about yourself.

Do you promise to try this at the earliest opportunity?

We each face a choice of who is going to be in charge of what comes out of our mouths. We can make an effort each day to have the Lord choose our words. "Set a guard over my mouth, O Lord; keep watch over the door of my lips" (Psalm 141:3). Or we can turn to Satan, the only alternative, because the tongue "... is itself set on fire by hell" (James 3:6).

Name some instances when you let the Lord set a guard over your mouth.

Now name some when your mouth was set on fire by hell.

I HATE TO TELL YOU THIS

This chapter originally ended with the paragraph above, but I now feel compelled to add this embarrassing post script:

Yesterday morning I put the finishing touches on this chapter and then went into the kitchen to make lunch—actually to warm up a chicken and rice dish that my wife, Kim, had made the day before.

Without really looking, I reached on top of the microwave and knocked to the floor a cheese-serving tray made of glass that had been given us by a good friend. It smashed to pieces. Then in front of God, the Heavenly Host, and Kim, some words spewed from my lips that made the golfer mentioned at the beginning of this chapter sound like a choir boy.

It had been a long time since I'd uttered some of those things, and it seems I could have at least gotten it right on the very day I concentrated so much on the very subject of what people say.

Ouch!

Please say that I'm not the only one who's done this.

CHAPTER SEVENTEEN

Faith or Fear?

Have you ever confused Lubbock, Texas, with the Promised Land?

About the time I celebrated two years of sobriety, I was invited to interview for a job in Lubbock that would send my career in a new direction. Even though I'd never been to Texas or even stepped foot west of the Mississippi River, I thought of Lubbock as a promised land, of sorts.

I suspect, though, that among those with first-hand knowledge of that city, few, if any, would think of it in those terms.

Located on the high plains of West Texas, Lubbock is flat and arid. The frequent dust storms there occasionally mix with precipitation to cause mud to fall from the sky. Hail is also a problem and sometimes described in terms of softball size.

The names of places in West Texas give an accurate description of the region. Driving northwest out of Lubbock, here are some towns you would encounter:

Shallowater—This very optimistic claim as to the amount of water there must have come from the chamber of commerce.

Littlefield—With so little precipitation, the fields there would, of course, be quite small.

Sudan—It is probably no coincidence that the Nubian Desert is located in an African country of the same name. Friends recently told me that some missionaries we know were residing in a tent in Sudan. Honestly, I thought they were talking about the West Texas version.

Earth—This is what flies through the air and lands in Lubbock during dust storms. West Texans claim that this flying dirt comes from New Mexico, the neighboring state to the west. With so much landing in West Texas, you might expect that when you drive across the state line, you'd find nothing but a huge hole in the ground.

Muleshoe—That pretty well speaks for itself. For the uninformed, this town is also the home of the National Mule Monument.

Other municipalities with descriptive names close to Lubbock include Levelland, Brownfield, Plainview, and Hale Center (probably a misspelling for Hail Center).

Driving between these locations, you halfway expect to see Moses leading the children of Israel in their ongoing journey through the wilderness.

At the time the Lubbock opportunity came up, I was continuing to work as a print journalist in the Detroit area. I earlier assumed that journalism would be my life-long occupation. But approaching age 30, it seemed like every story I wrote was a re-run of something I'd already written—dozens of times, in fact. I also was growing weary of dealing with local politicians.

Maurice Hall, the minister at my church, told me about the job opening as Director of Public Information at Lubbock (Texas) Christian University. Such a position would allow me to use my journalism skills at a Christian institution.

Lubbock, however, was 1,450 miles away, a major obstacle for me.

I sent my resumé to the school and was invited for an interview. This would mean leaving the newspaper office on a Friday afternoon and getting on an airplane in Detroit, flying first to Dallas, then changing planes, and continuing west to Lubbock. The interview would be Saturday morning, and I'd fly home that afternoon.

The last time I'd been on an aircraft was more than six years earlier, going from Detroit to Nashville after a weekend of heavy drinking. We hit turbulence somewhere over Kentucky and were bouncing all over the place as we approached Nashville. Lightening flashed all around us.

I was terrified and vowed that if I somehow got on the ground safely, I never again would travel by air.

DREAD OF DISASTER

As you already know, my drinking led to symptoms of agoraphobia, and I lived with thoughts often described as "a fear of impending doom." Connected to this, it seemed certain that something horrible—complete insanity, catastrophe, or death via heart attack or some other means—would overtake me within the next moment.

The dreaded disaster never came to fruition. This reality,

however, never lessened the anxiety that it would occur within the next moment. If that sounds to you like irrational, out-of-whack thinking, you are correct. It was a horrible way to live.

It got to the point where I was afraid to go anywhere—or even leave my apartment. I would start to drive somewhere, such as a job interview, and anxiety would overtake me a short way down the road. I then would turn around and go home without having kept my appointment. Each such occurrence led to greater feelings of defeat.

I coped with this phobia via false courage provided by alcohol.

"The sorrows of those will increase who run after other gods," wrote David (Psalm 16:4) while aptly describing what happened to me.

Telling you about this all these years later, it seems surreal, almost as if I am explaining lunacy that occurred in the mind of someone else. It is clear to me now that my idol made me a slave to self-centered fear that paralyzed me.

Self-centered fear is the polar opposite of faith in God.

Once sober, I did not gain instant faith, and my phobia about driving did not go away immediately. Initially, I had anxieties about going even short distances but made myself move forward, usually praying about it both before and during the trip. I told myself that I would never again turn around and go home without having reached my destination.

With continuing victories in these efforts, I gained a measure of faith and confidence. Little by little and with the passage of two years, driving became less of a problem.

This brings us back to the job interview in Lubbock. My

apprehension about flying had grown deep roots in the years since my last flight. I had more anxiety about that proposed trip than I would today of flying in a rocket to the moon.

My minister friend gave me some biblical assurances and prayed for me, but my faith remained smaller than an ameba's navel. I knew that if I allowed fear to keep me from getting on a Texas-bound aircraft, it would add to my fear of flying in the future. In fact, I would probably never fly.

Of course, I fully realized that Lubbock was not the real Promised Land. This fact became increasingly more obvious as I gazed at some West Texas scenes in a travel guide, including a photo of the National Mule Monument.

I knew, though, that opportunities would present themselves in Texas that I then could not imagine. The alternative was to remain in the Detroit area and continue in a career that had lost its zest for me.

When the fateful afternoon arrived, a friend from the recovery group, Mauri, drove me toward the airport. As we got close, I could see the jets taking off. Still wearing some shackles from my slave-world perception of self, I simply could not picture myself being on board one of them.

"I'm not going!" I cried out in desperation.

"You'd better think about that," was all that Mauri said.

I sat there thinking about how many times irrational fears had prompted me to turn around and drive home in defeat.

WHERE WAS THEIR FAITH?

After their tumultuous journey of some two years, the children of Israel traveled from Graves of the Craving to Hazeroth and from there northward to Kadesh Barnea. This was located in the Desert of Paran in close proximity to the Promised Land, Canaan, a name for modern-day Palestine.[1]

This land flowing with milk and honey wasn't empty, though. A number of pagan tribes already lived there, and the Israelites would have to displace them in order to move in themselves. In this way, they would benefit from the labors of those earlier inhabitants who had built cities and cultivated the land.

Having witnessed the miracles God performed on their behalf both in Egypt and during their journey, the Israelites could rest assured that God would keep the promises He'd made and perform mighty works that would enable them to take possession of the Promised Land. (See Exodus 23:20-33.)

As an initial step, Moses sent one man from each of the 12 tribes of Israel into Canaan. Their mission was to bring back a report about the people living there, the land, and the produce.

Forty days later, they returned carrying pomegranates, figs, and a cluster of grapes so large that it hung on a pole that was carried by two of them.

Here is what they reported when they returned:

"We went into the land to which you sent us, and it does flow with milk and honey! Here is its fruit. But the people who live there are powerful, and the cities are fortified and very large" (Numbers 13:27-28).

With the report starting to take a negative direction, Caleb spoke up. "We should go up and take possession of the land, for we can certainly do it" (Numbers 13:30).

MAJORITY RULE?

But 10 of the spies had different opinions. Here are their statements, each followed by my comments.

"We can't attack those people; they are stronger than we are" (Numbers 13:31).

How did these nay-sayers know this? Did they arm-wrestle them? Even if the current residents of the Promised Land were, indeed, physically stronger and had superior weapons, the children of Israel could be guaranteed a great victory with God on their side. Their self-centered fear, however, gave them a deluded picture that would serve as their road map to self-destruction.

"All the people we saw there are of great size" (Numbers 13:32).

Were they bigger than God? No, but they were in the minds of these men.

"The land we explored devours those living in it" (Numbers 13:32).

If this was truly the case, why didn't it devour its current inhabitants? It is a lie, another manifestation of their self-centered fear.

"We seemed like grasshoppers in our own eyes, and we looked the same to them" (Numbers 13:33).

No wonder they thought the people were giants. Even a sparrow looks like a giant to a grasshopper.

In what way have you seemed like a grasshopper in your own eyes?

Besides that, how did they know how they looked through the eyes of the people in the land? They were judging their insides by the outsides of the residents of Canaan.

The negativity spread, and that night, "all the Israelites grumbled against Moses and Aaron" (Numbers 14:2).

Here's what they said:

"If only we had died in Egypt! Or in this desert!" (Numbers 14:2)

This "woe-is-me" notion reeks of self-pity and ingratitude.

"Why is the Lord bringing us to this land only to let us fall by the sword?" (Numbers 14:3)

They blasphemed by judging the motives of God and calling Him a liar. Don't forget, God already had promised them a victory.

"Our wives and children will be taken as plunder" (Numbers 14:3).

Another false prophecy with a horrible outcome.

"'Wouldn't it be better for us to go back to Egypt?' And they said to each other, 'We should choose a leader and go back to Egypt'" (Numbers 14:3-4).

Since their departure from slave life in Egypt, this was the fifth recorded time they brought up positive aspects of slave life in Egypt. The previous instances include the approach of Pharaoh's army at the Red Sea (Exodus 14:11-12); fear of starvation (Exodus 16:3); fear of dehydration (Exodus 17:3); and when they craved food from Egypt while complaining about manna (Numbers 11:4-6). Except for when they craved Egyptian food, their predictions of the imminent future were always death.

This self-centered fear that paralyzes sounds familiar to me. How about you? It does not need to be an event of great magnitude. It could be something as simple as being afraid to shake someone's hand or say hello to him or her for fear of rejection.

In what ways have you been paralyzed by self-centered fear?
Why is Satan the source of such fear?

Hearing the fear and negativity from the children of Israel, the leaders who had not lost their faith in God (Moses, Aaron, Joshua, and Caleb) implored the people to move forward. "Do not rebel against the Lord. And do not be afraid of the people of the land, because we will swallow them up. Their protection is gone, but the Lord is with us. Do not be afraid of them" (Numbers 14:9).

The children of Israel now had information on both sides and stood at the turning point. Were they willing to step forward in faith that God would lead them to victory? Or would they let their fear determine their direction?

Think of some instances where you have stood at a turning point between faith and fear.
Name a positive outcome. Name a negative one.

TEXAS BOUND?

Mauri and I continued toward the airport. I prayed and determined to continue putting one foot in front of the other, even if my legs were quaking in fear.

I checked in at the airport counter and deposited my suitcase there. He and I then walked toward the gate through security, which at that time simply included a hand-held metal detector being waved around us.

Soon, I was in line with others to board the aircraft. I turned around and tried to smile as I waved to Mauri. Moving ahead, I knew I soon would find myself facing the most difficult step, the one from the jet-way to the plane. If I did that, there would be no turning back.

I kept moving forward.

Then I made that one small step for this man but a giant leap toward my future.

It was a white-knuckle trip all of the way to Dallas, where I changed planes and headed west toward Lubbock. The second leg of the journey was a little easier. The interview went fine the next morning, and I was taken back to the Lubbock airport later that day.

Waiting in the terminal, I saw two men wearing cowboy hats and looking intently into a photo album. Naughty pictures? I wanted to see for myself so I walked around behind them. What I saw was another perspective on the culture into which I would soon relocate. They were looking at 8 ½" x 11" photos of bulls.

The flights back to Detroit were actually enjoyable. Mauri picked me up at the Detroit airport, and I was exhilarated by the fact that through the grace of God, I had faced my fears and made the trip successfully. Flying has since become routine.

The move did, indeed, turn out to offer opportunities I couldn't have imagined. They have included (through the grace of God) earning my M.A. and Ph.D., teaching communication classes at three universities, writing several books, teaching Bible classes at five churches, conducting addiction-recovery seminars in many states, and finally, meeting Kim at church in 1999 and marrying her a year and a half later.

I lived in Lubbock for nearly eight years but never did make the one-hour drive to see the National Mule Monument. If you ever get there to see it, please send me a postcard.

CHAPTER EIGHTEEN

"Early the next morning..."

NUMBERS 14:40

As a drunkard, mornings were never the best part of the day for me.

Upon awakening, I would start to feel the physical effects of my latest debacle even before my dry eyes cracked open. The back of my head throbbed; my mouth and throat were parched, and there was a general wooziness of mind and body.

Immediately, thoughts of guilt and regret would sweep over me.

As usual, I'd stayed longer, drank more, and spent more than I'd planned. Lighting up my first cigarette of the day before getting out of bed, I might marvel at a nearly empty pack that I'd purchased the previous night. I'd even smoked more than I wanted.

These things combined to bring on a hangover that was just

starting and which I knew would last for the better part of the day.

In this state of remorse, I would delve into the haze of the previous night, a retrospection that could go on for several hours. During the midst of another activity, something like a freeze frame would pop into my mind. A huge tip to a topless dancer. A post in the parking lot of a bar which I'd side-swiped with my car, creating some fresh abrasions on the passenger-side door. A new "best buddy" for an hour or two whose name I couldn't remember.

It was crystal clear from these next-morning memories that I'd done things I wouldn't normally. Even scarier than the things I could remember were the things I couldn't, such as how had I driven my car from Point A to Point B?

Prisons are full of people who lived like I did. Many committed crimes they usually wouldn't have due to impaired judgment brought on by alcohol and/or drugs. Other convicted felons have no memory of their crimes. In either case, the lives of these people—and their victims—are changed for the worst.

Gratefully, I didn't end up in prison. But in those years of worshipping the god of pleasure, I did things and made decisions I still regret. Some of them changed my life unalterably. These are consequences of that insane lifestyle brought on by my idolatry. There is no "morning after" pill that will change these things.

A card laid is a card played.

MEANWHILE, NEAR THE PROMISED LAND

Such was the case with the children of Israel.

"Early the next morning they went up toward the high hill

country. 'We have sinned,' they said. 'We will go up to the place the Lord promised'" (Numbers 14:40).

"The next morning" followed the night in which they judged God as wanting them dead, expressed a desire to be slaves in Egypt, and wished to jettison their leaders, Moses, Aaron, Caleb, and Joshua. Then, when these four men tried to change their minds, the children of Israel talked about killing them.

God said He was ready to destroy all of them, but Moses intervened on their behalf and God forgave their sins. (See Numbers 14:10-20.)

There would be consequences, however. In the words of the Almighty, "Not one of them will ever see the land I promised on oath to their forefathers. No one who has treated me with contempt will ever see it" (Numbers 14:23).

Rather, those age 20 and older would wander in the desert for the rest of their days and die there. The 10 spies who gave the negative report were stricken with a plague and died immediately.

When Moses relayed God's message to the people that disastrous night, "They mourned bitterly" (Numbers 14:39). Then it was the next morning when they confessed their sin and said they would go into the Promised Land.

Did they really repent from the heart or were these mere words?

True repentance involves Godly sorrow (II Corinthians 7:9-11) and a change in attitude that prompts one to change direction in life. Based on the actions that followed, their repentance reminds me of vows I made after waking up with the regrets of a horrible hangover and then getting drunk again the very next night.

Of their plan to enter the Promised Land, Moses told them,

> *This will not succeed! Do not go up, because the Lord is not with you. You will be defeated by your enemies, for the Amalekites and Canaanites will face you there. Because you have turned away from the Lord, he will not be with you and you will fall by the sword (Numbers 14:41-43).*

"Nevertheless, in their presumption, they went up toward the high hill country... Then the Amalekites and Canaanites who lived in that hill country came down and attacked them and beat them down all the way to Hormah" (Numbers 14:44-45).

What was their next logical move? (Or what are the possibilities for people in general who have gone wrong and are facing the consequences of their actions?)

They could...

1. Genuinely repent, do their best to grow spiritually and leave their future in God's hands; or
2. Stay in denial, persist in saying they were correct and continue on a course of self-destruction.

The children of Israel pursued the second possibility.

In what way have you followed in their footsteps by repenting only on the surface but continuing the same course of action?

Korah, a distant cousin to Moses and Aaron who wanted to take over the priesthood from Aaron, led a group of 250 men described as "well-known community leaders who had been appointed members of the council" (Numbers 16:2). Approaching Moses and Aaron, they stated, "You have gone too far! The whole community is holy, every one of them, and the Lord is with them.

Why then do you set yourselves above the Lord's assembly?" (Numbers 16:3)

In this brief quotation, their arrogance was apparent in at least two ways as they...

1. Declared who was holy. (Of course, it was not up to them to decide on matters of holiness; this is what God does.)
2. Alleged that the Lord was with them. (In other words, they knew what God was thinking.)

All of these so-called leaders died that day.

If this wasn't bad enough, the next day "the whole Israelite community" (Numbers 16:41) blamed Moses and Aaron for killing Korah and his followers. A plague then claimed the lives of 14,700 of them.

This was followed by the last recorded words from the people age 20 and up who'd wanted to turn their backs on God and go back to Egypt. "We will die! We are lost, we are all lost! Anyone who even comes near the tabernacle of the Lord will die. Are we all going to die?" (Numbers 17:12-13)

You know the answer.

Except for a listing found in Numbers 33 of all the places the children of Israel camped during their 38 years of wandering, there is no other record of what occurred. Their ignominious legacy is similar to that of any other number of people whose lives are going nowhere.

MOSES FAILS, TOO

All those needless years of wandering must have been a bitter pill for Moses. He no doubt had been anxious to enter the Promised Land himself. But because of the ongoing shortcomings of the Israelites, two years turned into 40.

Finally, after all the original Israelites age 20 and up were buried in the desert, Moses led their children into Kadesh Barnea. If this location sounds familiar, it is the same place they were camped decades earlier when Moses sent the 12 spies into the Promised Land.

It was there that things went downhill for Moses and Aaron.

First, their sister, Miriam, died and was buried. They undoubtedly grieved her loss. Here's what happened next:

> *Now there was no water for the community, and the people gathered in opposition to Moses and Aaron. They quarreled with Moses and said, "If only we had died when our brothers fell dead before the Lord! Why did you bring the Lord's community into this desert, that we and our livestock should die here? Why did you bring us up out of Egypt to this terrible place? It has no grain or figs, grapevines or pomegranates. And there is no water to drink!" (Numbers 20:2-5)*

If Yogi Berra had been there, he might have said, "This is déjà vu all over again!"

Moses sought the Lord's advice. He was told, "Take the staff, and you and your brother Aaron gather the assembly together. Speak to that rock before their eyes and it will pour out its water" (Numbers 20:8).

Moses and Aaron then gathered the people around them. Based on what came out of Moses's mouth, it seems quite certain that he...

1. was having a bad day;
2. was sick and tired of dealing with the whining Israelites

and,

3. had not read Dale Carnegie's book, *How to Win Friends and Influence People*.

The next words from Moses were: "Listen, you rebels..." (Numbers 20:10). This was not exactly a way for him to ingratiate himself to his audience.

It went downhill from there when Moses stated, "Must we bring you water out of this rock?" (Numbers 20:10)

Don't let that last sentence slip by you. The operative word there is "we." It refers to him and Aaron. Did they have the power to bring water out of the rock? Certainly not! What Moses did here was elevate himself and his brother to God status. Apparently, Aaron was on board with that statement.

Later writing about this, a Psalmist wrote, "They rebelled against the Spirit of God, and rash words came from Moses' lips" (Psalm106:33).

Moses then struck the rock twice with his staff rather than talking to it as per God's directions to him. This disobedience is a logical consequence of the arrogance demonstrated by Moses.

Just as the Israelites had earlier been held accountable for their own rash words, the same was true for Moses and Aaron.

God told them: "Because you did not trust in me enough to honor me as holy in the sight of the Israelites, you will not bring this community into the land I give them" (Numbers 20:12). In other words, both Aaron and Moses would have the same fate of those who had fallen dead during the wilderness wanderings. The Bible does not record any reaction from them, but surely it was a huge disappointment.

Departing from Kadesh Barnea, the Israelites went to Mount Hor, believed to be about a day's journey northward;[1] Aaron died and was buried there.

Prior to their crossing the Jordan River and entering the Promised Land, the Israelites were gathered around Moses in the desert for the farewell sermon or sermons that became the book of Deuteronomy. This book includes a restating of The Ten Commandments along with admonishments to honor God and avoid idolatry.

Deuteronomy also includes the following three references to what Moses said about being barred from the Promised Land:

Addressing the Israelites, Moses stated: "*Because of you* the Lord became angry with me also and said, 'You shall not enter it, either'" (Deuteronomy 1:37, emphasis mine).

A little later, Moses told the people that he had asked God to relent and let him go into the Promised Land. "*But because of you* the Lord was angry with me and would not listen to me" (Deuteronomy 3:26, emphasis mine).

Finally, Moses stated, "The Lord was angry with me *because of you*, and he solemnly swore that I would not cross the Jordan and enter the good land the Lord your God is giving you as your inheritance" (Deuteronomy 4:21, emphasis mine).

As you can see, Moses failed to take responsibility for his own actions and, instead, pointed a finger of blame at the children of Israel. There is no record that Moses ever repented.

Is this why Moses was only able see the Promised Land from the distance of the mountain on which he was buried? Would a change of heart have changed this? God only knows. But we can say this with certainty: Despite the fact that scripture asserts "Moses was a very humble man, more humble than anyone else on the face of the earth" (Numbers 12:3), he still fell short of the mark.

LIKE FATHER, LIKE SON

Although they were a new generation, the children of Israel were not new and improved.

You read above about what they said to Moses and Aaron after arriving at Kadesh Barnea and not finding water.

Then after burying Aaron at Mount Hor and moving southward,

> *The people grew impatient on the way; they spoke against God and against Moses, and said, "Why have you brought us up out of Egypt to die in the desert? There is no bread! There is no water! And we detest this miserable food!" (Numbers 21:4-5)*

The last stop before their launch into the Promised Land was at a place called Shittim. You would never know it from looking at it, but the name means "meadow of acacias."[2] (An acacia is a tree or shrub with clusters of white or yellow flowers.) It was there that "the men began to indulge in sexual immorality with Moabite women, who invited them to the sacrifices to their gods. So Israel joined in worshipping the Baal of Peor" (Numbers 25:1-3).

The biblical text leaves little to the imagination as to the extent of the immorality that occurred in the meadow of acacias. It even names names. Right in front of a large group of people, including Moses, an Israelite man named Zimri (a son of Salu, who led a Simeonite family) took a Moabite woman into a tent. She was Cozbi, daughter of a Midianite tribal chief.

Aaron's grandson, Phinehas, picked up a spear and followed them. Apparently, when he entered the tent, Zimri and Cozbi were not making cookies for Vacation Bible School.

"With one thrust he drove the spear through the two of them, the man of Israel and the woman, right through their private parts" (Numbers 25:8, *The Message*). If there was not a commotion in the tent before this occurred, there certainly was after. It is hard to imagine they died quickly.

Based on their worship of Baal, is it any wonder the Israelites on the verge of entering the Promised Land would fail once they got there? God told Moses it would happen. "These people will soon prostitute themselves to the foreign gods of the land they are entering. They will forsake me and break the covenant I made with them" (Deuteronomy 31:16).

This became apparent a generation later when Joshua made his farewell address to Israel's leaders before dying at age 110. "Now fear the Lord and serve him with all your faithfulness," he told them. "Throw away the gods your forefathers worshiped beyond the River and in Egypt and serve the Lord" (Joshua 24:14).

After all this time, God's chosen people still were burdened with the Egyptian and other idols that had been carried by their parents and forebears going back hundreds of years. (The river refers to the Euphrates where Abraham had lived and where his father, Terah, had worshipped idols.) (See Joshua 24:2.)

In what way do you continue to worship the idols of your parents and ancestors?

In the same address, Joshua added, "Throw away the foreign

gods that are among you and yield your hearts to the Lord, the God of Israel" (Joshua 24:23). Biblical scholars believe that he's again referring to the Egyptian idols or to those they'd picked up during military victories in Canaan.[3]

Continuing to read the Old Testament following the book of Joshua, you'll find continuing references to the Hebrews losing their spiritual focus and falling back into idolatry, always to their detriment.

AM I ANY BETTER?

Based on the influence of modern and post-modern thinking, it is easy to get the idea that we are evolving into a better, more civilized people than those who inhabited the earth earlier. Our slave-world culture tells us we're all basically good people. (Gods even!) And once society fixes a few more problems, we'll all live together peacefully in a big world village, join hands and sing "Kumbaya" in perfect harmony.

Do you believe this? I certainly don't. Our problem is that we reside in a fallen world polluted by Satan and his countless idols. As a result, mankind does not have the capability to fix mankind's problems.

It is as if we're all making a tenuous trip across the ocean in a huge boat. Besides frequent storms and even hurricanes that toss our vessel about and nearly capsize us, the hull of the boat frequently leaks. To keep us from sinking, some of us are baling out water, and others are trying to patch up the holes. Sometimes, we're successful, but in other cases, water continues to trickle in. In the midst of all this, two miniature geysers suddenly appear in the hull on the other side of the boat.

Ultimately, this vessel will share the same fate as the Titanic.

Do you agree that you and I are in the same boat with the children of Israel? How do you know this?

"For all have sinned and fall short of the glory of God," wrote Paul (Romans 3:23). You know how I have fallen short while putting the finishing touches on this book.

How have you fallen short lately?

The solution for Paul and for us is discussed in the concluding chapter that follows.

CHAPTER NINETEEN

Our Key to Getting There

Do you remember Randall Lee Church? He's the prison inmate you met in the Introduction who'd served 27 ½ years and was released to a world that had moved forward without him. Baffled in his new surroundings, he yearned for the less complicated environment to which he was accustomed. That's how he set himself up for failure.

In answer to a letter from me, here's what Randall wrote from prison as this book was going to press:

> *I sit here every day and ask myself why after all those years would I blow a chance at freedom. And at first, I couldn't come up with an answer, but ... I had been here since I was 18 years old, so this was all I knew, so I came back. Do I want to be free? Yes! And I will be free in a few years, hopefully sooner than later. It's not that I couldn't adapt, but I was having trouble trying to adapt so I gave up, because it is so much easier in here. It's hard out there, and I'll be the first to admit it... Do I want to be in prison? No! I hate this place, but*

I've gotten used to it and I've gotten comfortable. Who wouldn't? Tomorrow I'll be 47, and I've never even had a drivers' license.

Randall's situation reminds me of the hopelessness described by Paul nearly 2,000 years ago.

"For I have the desire to do what is good, but I cannot carry it out. For what I do is not the good I want to do; no, the evil I do not want to do—this I keep on doing" (Romans 7:18-19). He continued, "What a wretched man I am!" (Romans 7:24)

Based on his own merits, Paul knew he could waste his life wandering aimlessly and without hope somewhere between the land of slavery and the Promised Land.

In what way are you and I in a similar situation today?

After his admission of personal powerlessness, Paul asked *the* question, "Who will rescue me from this body of death?" (Romans 7:24)

His answer: "Thanks be to God through Jesus Christ our Lord" (Romans 7:25). He added, "There is now no condemnation for those who are in Christ Jesus" (Romans 8:1).

Jesus does for us what we cannot do for ourselves.

Does Randall know this now? Yes. He wrote, "I need a positive surrounding like a Christian halfway house." He also mentioned a need to become involved with the 12 steps to recovery that were formulated by the program of Alcoholics Anonymous.

What Randall didn't know when he wrote that letter is that I already had sent him some material to get him started.

ANOTHER IDOL

It is an idol—the worship of self—that gives people notions that they have the power to earn entry to the Promised Land based on their own merits or best intentions.

This idol of self-sufficiency needs to be smashed.

What is the source of this idol?

How has it been a part of your belief system?

How do you rid yourself of it?

Jesus is the key. Through Him, we have access to the Promised Land. "Let us throw off everything that hinders and the sin that so easily entangles, and let us run with perseverance the race marked out for us. Let us fix our eyes on Jesus, the author and perfecter of our faith" (Hebrews 12:1-2).

In what ways are your wilderness-wandering days behind you with Jesus leading the way?

IT'S PERSONAL

I write this chapter after having been sober and seeking the Lord more than 38 years. Recall, though, in the midst of drunkenness some four decades ago, I professed to be an atheist. The thought processes behind this belief did not disappear automatically when I stopped drinking. While I did retain some earlier Bible knowledge, its only use to me at that time would have been in a game like Trivial Pursuit. I had zero faith in God.

When I left the mental hospital, my only hope for the future came from my fellow patient who said my solution might include abstaining from alcohol and attending recovery meetings.

It was at those get-togethers that I learned my sobriety was contingent on my relationship with God. The group did not define God for me. Rather, I had to find "God as I understood Him."

This was a good starting point because:

(1) I would have rebelled at people trying to force their religion on me, and

(2) Where else could I start in my understanding of God but at the bottom rung of spiritual maturity where I stood at that time?

By staying sober and attending meetings, I recognized that the spiritual principles advocated by the group came straight from the Bible. I started reading it, this time with a new eye.

My faith in God started to grow, and I began to see something in religion that had eluded me earlier: There were actual benefits right here and now to living a Godly life. I had earlier bought into the slave-world lie that if I were pious enough and miserable enough during this lifetime, I would have the dubious pleasure of residing in Heaven with other such long-faced people.

I also found that church and recovery meetings complemented each other. On a daily basis, I could usually be found at one, the other, or both.

At church one Sunday when I was 11 years old, I had confessed my belief that Jesus was the Son of God, and I was baptized. I had walked forward to do this while the congregation was singing the hymn "Out of My Bondage." I had no idea about the nature of bondage or even what the word meant. Approaching my 28th birthday after starting back to church, I had first-hand experience in the horrors of bondage.

After some six months at my new church, I confessed to the congregation how I had gone wrong. This time the congregation was singing, "Just As I Am," and I knew why the message applied to me.

I was, indeed, growing spiritually. To be perfectly honest, though, I did not relate when people referred to Jesus as their personal savior. I knew the right words to describe what He had done for the world, but the true meaning of this did not seem to reside in my heart.

After moving to Lubbock, I had a one-on-one conversation with a minister on the topic of Jesus. I told him I believed in God but still wasn't sure how Jesus fit into the picture. I can't recall his answer, but it seemed like nothing more than an empty slogan.

About the same time, I heard another minister give a sermon on "The Perfect Propitiation," a phrase he used numerous times. I left there thinking his lesson would have been much more effective if he'd focused more on the meaning of the perfect propitiation and less on his use of alliteration. (Of course, I was probably guilty of judging him.)

FINDING MY SAVIOR

Continuing to seek, I found the answer in J. B. Phillips' *Your God is Too Small*, a book mentioned earlier. I've reproduced the important paragraph below. His writing is a bit weighty and ponderous, but if you are searching as I was, stick with it and pray about it.

Suppose now that God, who has become human and represents in one person both His own Godhood and Humanity, allows Himself, though personally guiltless, to be involved in the complex. God, now, who made the inexorable rules of cause and effect, deliberately exposes Himself to the consequences of the world's self-love and sin. Because He is God, to do such a thing once in time is indicative of an eternal attitude, and we view the Character of God in an entirely different light if we see Him not abrogating justice, not issuing a mandate of reversal of natural law and order, but overcoming a repugnance which we cannot begin to imagine by letting Himself be Representative Man and suffering in His own Person the logical and inevitable suffering and death which the world has earned. The Moral Perfection which a man quite rightly dreads, has deliberately consented to become under the limitations of humanity, the focal point of the assault of evil. We cannot imagine what this would involve, but even to begin to think that it might be true takes the breath away.[1]

When I let this sink in, the following words cried out by Jesus from the cross took on a new meaning: "My God, my God, why have you forsaken me?" (Matthew 27:46)

It is generally understood that in a spiritual sense, these words reveal that God had turned His back on His own son.

Here is the biblical logic behind this idea:

Referring to Jesus, Paul wrote, "God made him who had no sin to be sin for us, so that in him we might become the righteousness of God" (II Corinthians 5:21).

The Apostle Peter wrote of Jesus on the cross, "He himself bore our sins in his body on the tree... by his wounds you have been healed" (I Peter 2:24).

The prophet Habakkuk wrote of God, "Your eyes are too pure

to look on evil; you cannot tolerate wrong" (Habakkuk 1:13).

Putting this together, sinless Jesus carried our sins/idols/ gods to the cross, and we ended up 100% spiritually sound in the process, thus opening up the door for us to the Promised Land. Since God cannot look on evil, He had to turn away from His son.

Well-meaning teachers sometimes focus solely on the physical aspects of the crucifixion. They miss the point, however, because the enormity of the sacrifice lay in its spiritual ramifications. Here we have Jesus, a part of God, taking our sins on Himself. This separated Him from God, His own very nature. This would create the type of pain to which Phillips referred when writing, "We cannot imagine what this would involve, but even to begin to think that it might be true takes the breath away."[2]

Despite my years of blasphemy, utter selfishness, and the heartless treatment of others, Jesus became my personal savior because He gave me the greatest possible gift—eternal life. It is the ultimate in gifts because the value of each of our souls is more than the sum total of all riches on earth. (See Matthew 16:26 and Mark 8:35-36.)

My ugly slate was wiped clean. I am a new creation in Christ. This has huge implications in my life, including my perspective of God, other people, and my role on this earth. (See II Corinthians 5:1– 6:2.)

What are the implications in your life of being a new creation in Christ?

The death of Jesus on the cross destroyed "him who holds the power of death—that is, the devil"—and freed "those who all their lives were held in slavery by their fear of death" (Hebrews 2:14-15).

The gift from Jesus is truly the only one that keeps on giving—forever.

What, if anything, is holding you back from knowing Jesus as your personal savior?

MOSES KNEW

In his message to the children of Israel near the end of his life, Moses told them that Jesus would be coming.

This prophecy starts out, "The Lord your God will raise up for you a prophet like me from among your own brothers. You must listen to him" (Deuteronomy 18:15). This indicates that like Moses, Jesus would be from the seed of Abraham (Jewish). Besides that, the lives of Moses and Jesus had many parallels. See the adjoining chart, "Some Comparisons Between Jesus and Moses."

While the life of Moses provided kind of a sneak preview of Jesus, a huge difference between them is that Moses was a *servant* of God and Jesus is the *son* of God (Hebrews 3:5-6, emphases mine).

Quoting God, the prophecy of Moses continued:

> *I will raise up for them a prophet like you from among their brothers; I will put my words in his mouth, and he will tell them everything I command him. If anyone does not listen to my words that the prophet speaks in my name, I myself will call him to account (Deuteronomy 18:18-19).*

"The prophet" to which Moses refers is the promise of the forthcoming Messiah, a name which means "anointed one."[3] Based on this, the Jews anticipated his arrival.[4]

In the New Testament, there are several references to Jesus as the long-awaited prophet. (See John 1:6-34; 6:14; 7:40; Acts 3:18-23.)

Conversing with some unbelieving Jews, Jesus stated, "If you believed Moses, you would believe me" (John 5:46).

A non-Jewish woman said to Jesus, "'I know that Messiah' (called Christ) 'is coming. When he comes, he will explain everything to us.' Then Jesus declared, 'I who speak to you am he'" (John 4:25-26).

Besides comparisons to Moses, huge events in the lives of the children of Israel were demonstrated in the life of Jesus.

For example, Jesus compared Himself to manna in the following passage while foreshadowing the role of the bread in Christian communion.

> *I am the bread of life. Your forefathers ate manna in the desert, yet they died. But here is the bread that comes down from heaven, which a man may eat and not die. I am the living bread that came down from heaven. If anyone eats of this bread, he will live forever. This bread is my flesh, which I will give for the life of the world (John 6:48-51).*

As God provided life-sustaining manna, Jesus supplies soul-saving sustenance on this journey and beyond.

OUR PASSOVER

There are also biblical comparisons between the Passover and Jesus.

The children of Israel had been spared the death of first-born sons because they followed God's command to smear the blood of

Some Comparisons Between Moses and Jesus[7]

MOSES	JESUS
Law-Giver *Exodus 34:32*	Law-Giver *Hebrews 8:6,10,13*
Deliverer from bondage in Egypt *Exodus 14:21-22*	Deliverer from bondage of sin *Romans 7:23-25*
Builder of Tabernacle *Exodus 39:32*	Builder of Church *Matthew 16:18*
Intercessor *Exodus 32:10*	Intercessor *Romans 8:34*
Shepherd *Exodus 3:1; Psalm 77:20*	Shepherd *John 10:11*
Transfigured *Exodus 34:29; Luke 9:30*	Transfigured *Luke 9:29*
Descendant of Abraham, born in a country under a Gentile king *Exodus 1:8 – 2:10*	Descendant of Abraham, born in a country under a Gentile king *Luke 1:4-7*
Saved from Pharaoh's edict to kill all newborn Hebrew boys *Exodus 1:22*	Saved from Herod's edict to kill all newborn Hebrew boys *Matthew 2:13-16*
Brought up in a household where the man was not his actual father *Exodus 2:10*	Brought up in a household where the man was not his actual father *Matthew 1: 18-25*
Subject of criticism from family and Israelites *Exodus 5:19-21; Numbers 12:1-2*	Subject of criticism from family and Israelites *John 7:3-5; 12:34-37*
Went on a 40-day fast *Exodus 34:28*	Went on a 40-day fast *Matthew 4:1-2*
Sent out 12 men with an assignment *Numbers 13:1-15*	Sent out 12 men with an assignment *Matthew 10:1-16*
God spoke to him audibly *Exodus 19:9-10*	God spoke to him audibly *John 12:23-30*

one-year-old lambs or goats on their doorposts. (See Exodus 12:1-13.) Along with unleavened (made without yeast) bread, the meat from these slaughtered animals were a part of the first Jewish Passover Feast, which has been commemorated annually since then.

Jesus was referred to as "the Lamb of God, who takes away the sin of the world" (John 1:29) and the "Passover Lamb" who "has been sacrificed" (I Corinthians 5:7).

What we know as "The Last Supper" occurred when Jesus celebrated Passover with His apostles just prior to His crucifixion. Jesus broke the bread and said, "This is my body given for you; do this in remembrance of me" (Luke 22:19). After the supper, Jesus held a cup of wine and told them to drink from it. "This cup is the new covenant in my blood, which is poured out for you" (Luke 22:20).

As a part of the new covenant to which Jesus referred, the Jewish Passover Feast became communion in the Christian era. Rather than using an actual lamb, we celebrate Jesus as the sacrificial lamb who died for our sins. "For whenever you eat this bread and drink this cup, you proclaim the Lord's death until he comes" (I Corinthians 11:26).

Moses's instructions for the original Passover Feast stand as prophecies that apply to Jesus.

For example, the Israelites were told to select lambs without defect (Exodus 12:5). Jesus was sinless (Hebrews 4:15).

When the children of Israel were preparing the lambs for the first Passover, they were instructed to break none of their bones (Exodus 12:46). None of Jesus's bones were broken during His crucifixion (John 19:31-37).

The Israelites were instructed to use a hyssop plant to smear the blood of a lamb on their door frames (Exodus 12:22). Just before the death of Jesus on the cross, a hyssop plant was used to lift a sponge that had been soaked in wine vinegar to quench His thirst (John 19:29).

What Christians know as Good Friday, the day of Jesus's crucifixion, also marks the first day of Passover.

According to Rabbi Jonathan Bernis, Jesus was crucified at the very hour when the Jews of His day were killing their lambs. The resurrection of Jesus on what we know as the first Easter Sunday corresponds with the Jewish Feast of First Fruits.[5]

With the death of Jesus on the cross, He became the ultimate sacrifice once and for all. According to Paul, "The risen Jesus is at the right hand of God and is also interceding for us" (Romans 8:34).

In short, when Jesus goes to bat for us, God sees us not according to our many spiritual failures but as people with a clean slate. "As far as the east is from the west, so far has he removed our transgressions from us" (Psalm 103:12).

AN EARLY NEED

Paul tried to get it right but couldn't. The same is true for you and me. Even Moses failed. We're all separated from God on the basis of our own poor choices. As mentioned in the previous chapter, that accounts for all of us residing in a fallen world.

It hasn't always been this way, though.

Our greatest grandparents, Adam and Eve, had a face-to-face relationship with their Creator and apparently would reside with Him forever in the Garden of Eden, a perfect place God had created.

Through their choice to go for Satan's temptation to have an eye-opening experience and become like God, sin entered the world (Genesis 3:1-8).

For the part Adam played in this, God said to him, "By the sweat of your brow you will eat your food until you return to the ground, since from it you were taken; for dust you are and to dust you will return" (Genesis 3:19).

In other words, Adam would die, and so would all of his ancestors. Sin and death are the inevitable results of Satan's entry here. Our fallen world is a result of the ongoing presence of the devil.

Spelling out the consequences for Satan's part in the fall of humanity, God said, "I will put enmity between you and the woman, and between your offspring and hers; he will crush your head, and you will strike his heel" (Genesis 3:15).

That woman was Eve, and generations later, the offspring of woman was Jesus. The offspring of Satan are those who "seek to oppose God's purposes in creation and redemption."[6]

The evil one did "strike" Jesus on the heel in that He suffered a mortal wound on the cross and died like the rest of Adam's ancestors. Unlike the rest of us, though, Jesus came back to life in bodily form. He overcame death and defeated Satan, thus crushing his head.

Satan's influence of evil continues but is temporary. Though we will die, we are saved from the second death, also known as hell (Revelation 20:11-15), through Christ and will join Him in

Heaven. We then will be restored to the face-to-face relationship with God that once was enjoyed by Adam and Eve.

As prophesied by the Apostle John,

> *Now the dwelling of God is with men, and he will live with them. They will be his people, and God himself will be with them and be their God. He will wipe every tear from their eyes. There will be no more death or mourning or crying or pain, for the old order of things has passed away (Revelation 21:3-4).*

Referring to Heaven, John continued:

> *I did not see a temple in the city, because the Lord God Almighty and the Lamb are its temple. The city does not need the sun or the moon to shine on it, for the glory of God gives it light, and the Lamb is its lamp. The nations will walk by its light, and the kings of the earth will bring their splendor into it. On no day will its gates ever be shut, for there will be no night there. The glory and honor of the nations will be brought into it. Nothing impure will ever enter it, nor will anyone who does what is shameful or deceitful, but only those whose names are written in the Lamb's book of life (Revelation 21:22-26).*

Who's writing the names in that book?

Our Savior! He's the One who shatters the idols that bind us so that we may escape the bondage of self and enter victoriously into the Promised Land.

Endnotes

Introduction

1. Jazmine Ulloa, "Convict Couldn't Handle Being Free," *The San Antonio Express News*, Sept. 25, 2011, 1-B, 4-B.
2. Associated Press, "Freed Inmate Burns House So He Can Go Back to Jail," *Dallas Morning News*, Sept. 26, 2011, 3-A.
3. Ulloa, *op. cit.*
4. *ibid.*
5. Associated Press, *op. cit.*

Chapter 2

1. The Shema (Deuteronomy 6: 4-5) is the center-piece of Jewish daily prayer service and taught to children to say before they go to bed at night. (http://en.wikipedia.org/wiki/Shema_Yisrael) As found in Matthew 22:37, when asked by a Pharisee about the greatest commandment, Jesus quoted Deuteronomy 6:5.
2. Sources for this myth include http://en.wikipedia.org/wiki/Horus, http://www.thekeep.org/~kunoichi/kunoichi/themestream/sexuality.html and http://en.wikipedia.org/wiki/Set_(mythology).
3. Geraldine Pinch, *Egyptian Mythology: A Guide to the Gods, Goddesses, and Traditions of Ancient Egypt*, Oxford University Press, Oxford, UK, 2002, 178.
4. Pinch, *op. cit.*
5. http://www.ancientegyptonline.co.uk/.
6. John J. Davis, *Moses and the Gods of Egypt: Studies in Exodus, Second Edition*, BMH Books, Winona Lake, IN, 2006, 94.
7. Davis, *op. cit.*, 95.
8. Bruce Feiler, *Walking the Bible: A Journey by Land Through the Five Books of Moses*, Harper Perennial, New York, 2005, 131.
9. Three other reasons to conclude the children of Israel had maintained their spiritual heritage from the Patriarchs include: (1) The Israelites had continued the rite of male circumcision established centuries earlier as a part of God's covenant with Abraham (Genesis 17:11-14; Joshua 5:4-8); (2) Hebrew midwives were ordered by Pharaoh to kill baby boys who were born. "The Midwives, however, feared God and did not do what the king of Egypt had told them..." (Exodus 1:17); (3) The Israelites had maintained their tribal identities. See Numbers 1 and 2.)

Chapter 3

1. J. D. Douglas and Merrill C. Tenney, *The New International Dictionary of the Bible*, Zondervan, Grand Rapids, MI, 1987, 424.

Chapter 4

1. Timothy Keller, *Counterfeit Gods: The Empty Promises of Money, Sex, and Power, and the Only Hope That Matters*, Dutton, New York, 2009, xvii.
2. Elyse Fitzpatrick, *Idols of the Heart: Learning to Long for God Alone,* P&R Publishing, Phillipsburg, NJ, 2001, 117.

3. Fitzpatrick, *op. cit.*, 25.
4. *ibid.*
5. Dan B. Allender and Tremper Longman III, *Breaking the Idols of Your Heart: How to Navigate the Temptations of Life*, IVP Books, Downers Grove, IL, 14.
6. Keller, *op. cit.*, 169-170.
7. *ibid.*
8. Keller, *op. cit.*, 64.
9. Keller, *op. cit.*, 64-65.
10. Keller, *op. cit.*, 65.
11. *ibid.*
12. *ibid.*
13. Fitzpatrick, *op. cit.*, 25.
14. Keller, *op. cit.*, 3.

Chapter 5

1. Mark Driscoll, *Doctrine: What Christians Should Believe*, Crossway Books, Wheaton, IL, 2010, 337- 338.
2. http://www.tamu.edu/faculty/choudhury/culture.html.
3. Edward T. Hall, *The Silent Language*, New York: Doubleday & Co., 1959, 39.
4. http://en.allexperts.com/q/Management-Consulting-2802/2009/7/Consumer-Behaviour-2.htm.
5. http://sportsillustrated.cnn.com/vault/article/magazine/MAG1152110/4/index.htm.
6. http://www.bamafootball4life.com/2010/12/nick-saban-the-six-million-dollar-man/.
7. Bruce Feiler, *Walking the Bible: A Journey by Land Through the Five Books of Moses*, Harper Perennial, New York, 2005, 131.
8. John R. Diggs, Jr., M.D., "The Health Risks of Gay Sex," http://www.catholiceducation.org/articles/homosexuality/ho0075.htm.
9. *Leonard Maltin's 2012 Movie Guide*, Signet, New York, 2011, 1540.
10. http://www.physorg.com/news/2011-03-lingering-seeds-sexual-revolution.html.
11. Josh McDowell and Bob Hostetler, *The New Tolerance: How a Cultural Movement Threatens to Destroy You, Your Faith, and Your Children,* Tyndale House Publishers, Wheaton, IL, 1998, 32.
12. McDowell and Hostetler, *op. cit.*, 35.
13. http://www.leaderu.com/orgs/probe/docs/spelltru.html.
14. *ibid.*
15. McDowell and Hostetler, *op. cit.*, 36.
16. Paul C. Vitz, *Psychology as Religion: The Cult of Self-Worship, Second Edition*, William B. Eerdmans Publishing Co., Grand Rapids, MI, 1994, xvi.
17. Eric L. Johnson, "A Brief History of Christians in Psychology," in *Psychology & Christianity: Five Views, Second Edition*, Eric L. Johnson (editor), InterVarsity Press, Downers Grove, IL, 2010, 10.
18. McDowell and Hostetler, *op. cit.*, 36.
19. Gene Edward Veith, Jr., *Postmodern Times; A Christian Guide to Contemporary Thought and Culture*, Crossway Books, Wheaton, IL, 1994, 15.
20. McDowell and Hostetler, *op. cit.*, 39.
21. Veith, *op. cit.,* 16.

Chapter 6
1. John J. Davis, *Moses and the Gods of Egypt: Studies in Exodus, Second Edition*, BMH Books, Winona Lake, IN, 2006, 98.
2. Davis, *op. cit.*, 102.
3. Geraldine Pinch, *Egyptian Mythology: A Guide to the Gods, Goddesses, and Traditions of Ancient Egypt*, Oxford University Press, Oxford, UK, 2002, 3.
4. *ibid.*
5. Davis, *op. cit.*, 102.
6. Davis, *op. cit.*, 149.
7. J. B. Phillips, *Your God is Too Small*, Touchstone, New York, 1997, 7.
8. Davis, *op. cit.,* Pinch, *op. cit.*, http://en.wikipedia.org/wiki/Dung_beetle; http://www.touregypt.net/featurestories/bull.htm; http://en.wikipedia.org/wiki/Nut_(goddess); http://hubpages.com/hub/Ten-Plagues-For-Ten-Gods; www.padfield.com/acrobat/history/gods_of_egypt.pdf.
9. Davis, *op. cit.*, 107.
10. Pinch, *op. cit.,* 182.
11. http://hubpages.com/hub/Ten-Plagues-For-Ten-Gods.

Chapter 7
1. Rabbi Yoseph Kahanov, Jacksonville, FL, "Self-Destructive Arrogance: The Tendency To Cut The Nose To Spite The Face," Jan. 22, 2010, http://www.collive.com/show_news.rtx?id=7371&hl=berel.
2. John J. Davis, *Moses and the Gods of Egypt: Studies in Exodus, Second Edition*, BMH Books, Winona Lake, IN, 2006, 111.
3. www.padfield.com/acrobat/history/gods_of_egypt.pdf.
4. Davis, *op. cit.*
5. Davis, *op. cit.*, 115.
6. Davis, *op. cit.*
7. Davis, *op. cit.*, 121.
8. www.padfield.com/acrobat/history/gods_of_egypt.pdf.
9. Davis, *op. cit.*, 124.
10. Davis, *op. cit.*
11. Davis, *op. cit.*, 126.
12. Davis, *op. cit.*, 128.
13. Davis, *op. cit.*, 129.
14. Davis, *op. cit.*, 136.
15. http://hubpages.com/hub/Ten-Plagues-For-Ten-Gods.

Chapter 8
1. http://www.sage.edu/faculty/salomd/ld/egypt.html.
2. Rabbi Yoseph Kahanov, Jacksonville, FL, "Self-Destructive Arrogance: The Tendency To Cut The Nose To Spite The Face," Jan. 22, 2010, http://www.collive.com/show_news.rtx?id=7371&hl=berel.

Chapter 9
1. Bruce Feiler, *Walking the Bible: A Journey by Land Through the Five Books of Moses*, Harper Perennial, New York, 2005, 200.
2. Feiler, *op. cit.* 222-223.
3. Jeff Manion, *The Land Beween: Finding God in Difficult Transitions,* Zondervan, Grand Rapids, MI, 2010, 20-21.

4. Jack Zavata, Why Change is So Hard: Managing Change - Why Change is So Hard and What to Do About It," http://christianity.about.com/od/topicaldevotions/a/whychangeishard.htm.
5. *Alcoholics Anonymous: The Story of How Many Thousands of Men and Women Have Recovered from Alcoholism, Third Edition,* Alcoholics Anonymous World Services, Inc., New York, 1976, 60.
6. Feiler, *op. cit.*, 81.

Chapter 10

1. *The Family Worship Bible*, Holman Bible Publishers, Nashville, 1991, 214.
2. http://en.wikipedia.org/wiki/Ebers_Papyrus.
3. *ibid.*
4. S. I. McMillen and David E. Stern, *None of These Diseases: The Bible's Health Secrets for the 21st Century*, Fleming H. Revell, Grand Rapids, Michigan, 2000, 9.
5. McMillen and Stern, *op. cit.*, 10.
6. *ibid.*
7. McMillen and Stern, *op. cit.*, 24-25.
8. Jonathan Wells, *Icons of Evolution: Science or Myth? Why Much of What We Teach About Evolution Is Wrong*, Regnery Publishing, Inc., Washington, D.C., 2000.
9. http://www.depressionperception.com/stress/stress_facts_and_statistics.asp.
10. http://www.dealwithstress.com/What-Are-The-Physical-Illnesses-Related-To-Stress-.html and http://www.mayoclinic.com/health/stress/AN01286.
11. http://www.depressionperception.com/stress/stress_facts_and_statistics.asp.
12. Kenneth L. Boles, *The College Press NIV Commentary—Galatians & Ephesians*, College Press Publishing Co., Joplin, MO, 1993, 319.
13. http://www.everydayhealth.com/longevity/can-promiscuity-threaten-longevity.aspx.
14. Karen Testerman, http://www.abortiontv.com/Avoid!/std.htm.
15. *ibid.*
16. Testerman, *op. cit.* and http://www.everydayhealth.com/longevity/can-promiscuity-threaten-longevity.aspx.
17. Testerman, *op. cit.* and John R. Diggs, Jr., M.D., "The Health Risks of Gay Sex," http://www.catholiceducation.org/articles/homosexuality/ho0075.htm.
18. "Obesity Debate: Should individuals, or government, take aim?" *The Dallas Morning News*, Aug. 7, 2011, p. 11-A and http://www.ehd.org/health_obesity.php.
19. http://en.wikipedia.org/wiki/Obesity.
20. *ibid.*
21. *ibid.*

Chapter 11

1. J. D. Douglas and Merrill C. Tenney, *The New International Dictionary of the Bible*, Zondervan, Grand Rapids, MI, 1987, 620.
2. *ibid.*
3. Bruce Feiler, *Walking the Bible: A Journey by Land Through the Five Books of Moses*, Harper Perennial, New York, 2005, 220.

Chapter 12

1. http://www.pbs.org/wgbh/pages/frontline/shows/justice/etc/script.html.
2. http://www.touregypt.net/featurestories/bull.htm.
3. *ibid.*
4. http://www.godrules.net/library/clarke/clarkeexo32.htm.
5. http://bible.cc/exodus/32-6.htm.
6. John J. Davis, *Moses and the Gods of Egypt: Studies in Exodus, Second Edition*, BMH Books, Winona Lake, IN, 2006, 293.
7. *NIV Archaeological Study Bible*, Zondervan, Grand Rapids, MI, 2005, 142.
8. http://bible.cc/exodus/32-35.htm.
9. http://mb-soft.com/believe/txc/syncreti.htm.
10. http://www.buzzle.com/articles/syncretism-examples.html.
11. http://worldviewchurch.org/worldview-challenge/28-guard-against-syncretism.
12. http://www.equip.org/articles/yoga-exercises-and-christianity.
13. http://mb-soft.com/believe/txc/syncreti.htm.
14. Dr. Gailyn Van Rheenen, "Worldview and Syncretism," Paper presented at the Symposium, Distinctively Christian, Distinctly Mongolian, Ulaanbaatar, Mongolia, March 11, 2003.
15. *ibid.*
16. Caroline Seawright. "Ancient Egyptian Sexuality," http://www.touregypt.net/featurestories/sexuality.htm.

Chapter 13

1. http://www.godrules.net/library/clarke/clarkegen2.htm.
2. http://en.wikipedia.org/wiki/Agoraphobia.
3. William Kirk Kilpatrick, *Psychological Seduction: The Failure of Modern Psychology*, Thomas Nelson Publishers, Nashville, 1983, 23.
4. *ibid.*
5. Gary L. Almy, M.D., *How Christian Is Christian Counseling: The Dangerous Secular Influences That Keep Us from Caring for Souls*, Crossway Books, Wheaton, IL, 2000, 33.
6. Paul C. Vitz, *Psychology as Religion: The Cult of Self-Worship*, 2nd Edition, William B. Eerdmans Publishing Co., Grand Rapids, MI, 1994, xii.
7. Martin and Deidre Bobgan, *Psycho Heresy: The Psychological Seduction of Christianity*, East Gate Publishers, Santa Barbara, CA, 1987.
8. Almy, *op. cit.*, 27.
9. Chris Tucker, "Addiction and Genius," *The Dallas Morning News,* Aug 28, 2011, 6-E.
10. http://www.beliefnet.com/Entertainment/2000/03/The-Assisted-Suicide-Of-Sigmund-Freud.aspx.
11. http://www.beliefnet.com/Entertainment/2000/03/The-Assisted-Suicide-Of-Sigmund-Freud.aspx.
12. http://www.the-tribulation-network.com/denemcgriff/Apostasy/recognizing_deception_and_apostasy.htm.
13. Bobgan, *op. cit.*, 5.
14. Bobgan, *op. cit.*, 12.
15. Bobgan, *op. cit.*, 67.
16. David M. Tyler, *God's Funeral: Psychology—Trading the Sacred for the Secular*, Focus Publishing, Bemidji. MN, 2009, 54-55.

Chapter 15
1. *The Family Worship Bible*, Holman Bible Publishers, Nashville, 1991, 307.
2. http://bible.cc/numbers/11-4.htm.
3. *Webster's Collegiate Dictionary, Fifth Edition*, G. & C. Merriam Co, Springfield, MA, 1947, 237.
4. Jeff Manion, *The Land Beween: Finding God in Difficult Transitions,* Zondervan, Grand Rapids, MI, 2010, 36.
5. Manion, *op. cit.,* 37.
6. www.ncada-stl.org/.../some_things_you_should_know_about_cocaine.pdf.

Chapter 17
1. J. D. Douglas and Merrill C. Tenney, *The New International Dictionary of the Bible*, Zondervan, Grand Rapids, MI, 1987, 188.

Chapter 18
1. J. D. Douglas and Merrill C. Tenney, *The New International Dictionary of the Bible*, Zondervan, Grand Rapids, MI, 1987, 449.
2. Douglas and Tenney, *op. cit.*, 939.
3. http://bible.cc/joshua/24-23.htm.

Chapter 19
1. J. B. Phillips, *Your God is Too Small*, Touchstone, New York, 1997, 106.
2. *ibid.*
3. J. D. Douglas and Merrill C. Tenney, *The New International Dictionary of the Bible*, Zondervan, Grand Rapids, MI, 1987, 644.
4. Most Jews today reject the idea of Jesus as the Messiah. Some believe there never will be a Messiah and that it is imperative that Jewish people work together to bring about a utopian existence which will be a type of "Messianic Age." (http://en.wikipedia.org/wiki/Jewish_messianism). Other Jewish people believe that Messiah is yet to come and that "the conduct of mankind will determine the time of the mashiach's (Messiah's) coming... (such as) when he is most needed (because the world is so sinful), or in a time when he is most deserved (because the world is so good)." This group expects the Messiah "will bring about the political and spiritual redemption of the Jewish people by bringing (them) back to Israel and restoring Jerusalem (Isaiah 11:11-12; Jeremiah 23:8; 30:3; Hosea 3:4-5) (and that) He will establish a government in Israel that will be the center of all world government, both for Jews and Gentiles." (Isaiah 2:2-4; 11:10; 42:1). (http://www.jewfaq.org/mashiach.htm).
5. Rabbi Jonathan Bernis, *A Rabbi Looks at Jesus of Nazareth*, Chosen Books, Bloomington, MN, 2010, 63.
6. Henry Morris, *The Genesis Record: A Scientific and Devotional Commentary on the Book of Beginnings*, Baker Book House, Grand Rapids, MI, 2000, 121.
7. For a more comprehensive listing of comparisons, see http://www.osyministries.com/index.php?option=com_content&view=article&catid=44%3Aosy-study-docs&id=202%3Aparallels-between-moses-and-the-messiah&Itemid=87.

Acknowledgments

Thanks to my wife, Kim. Without her support, much of my ministry would not be possible. She also made many helpful suggestions in the final stages of the manuscript.

Gratitude goes to the following four Sunday morning classes at our church home, the Prestoncrest Church of Christ in Dallas, Texas, where I taught this material as I was writing this book: Living Faith, Friendship, Single Purpose, and Brothers' Keepers. Their suggestions, questions, and comments guided me in honing this material into its present form.

Special thanks to Bill Jones, whose comment helped me realize that the children of Israel are not simply bad examples; rather, they are just like the rest of us.

Kudos to Irene Swindell, Ron Black, Wayne Williams, Tim Price, and my long-time friend from college, Denny Miller.

For help in the process of determining a title for this book, I am grateful to the Friendship Class at church, inmates at the Collin County Detention Center, and many of my Facebook friends.